S. HRG.

WILDFIRE MANAGEMENT

HEARING

BEFORE THE

COMMITTEE ON ENERGY AND NATURAL RESOURCES UNITED STATES SENATE

ONE HUNDRED TWELFTH CONGRESS

FIRST SESSION

TO

CONSIDER THE WILDFIRE MANAGEMENT PROGRAMS OF THE FEDERAL
LAND MANAGEMENT AGENCIES

JUNE 14, 2011

Printed for the use of the
Committee on Energy and Natural Resources

U.S. GOVERNMENT PRINTING OFFICE

70–919 PDF

WASHINGTON : 2011

For sale by the Superintendent of Documents, U.S. Government Printing Office
Internet: bookstore.gpo.gov Phone: toll free (866) 512–1800; DC area (202) 512–1800
Fax: (202) 512–2104 Mail: Stop IDCC, Washington, DC 20402–0001

CONTENTS

STATEMENTS

APPENDIX

WILDFIRE MANAGEMENT

Tuesday, June 14, 2011

U.S. SENATE,
COMMITTEE ON ENERGY AND NATURAL RESOURCES,
Washington, DC.

The committee met, pursuant to notice, at 10:03 a.m., in room SD–366, Dirksen Senate Office Building, Hon. Jeff Bingaman, chairman of the committee, presiding.

OPENING STATEMENT OF HON. JEFF BINGAMAN, U.S. SENATOR FROM NEW MEXICO

The CHAIRMAN. OK. Why do we not get started? The purpose of our hearing this morning is to consider the Federal land management agencies' wildfire management programs. I am going to give a short statement. Then Senator Murkowski will, and then we will hear from our colleague, Senator Kyl, before we hear from our two witnesses.

It has been a dynamic year of severe weather—intense tornadoes, flooding throughout much of the United States, extreme drought, and wildfire activity in the southwest and much of the south. The overall trend of increasing drought and wildfire in the west and southwest have been attributed by numerous scientific reports to climate change, including the recent report of our National Academy of Sciences entitled, "America's Climate Choices."

Since climate change will continue into the future, we can expect the incidence of severe weather and further drying out of the already arid regions of the west to continue as well. We had a hearing in Santa Fe about 6 weeks ago with some experts, and the point was made repeatedly that droughts will be more frequent in the southwest, and they will last longer than they have in the past.

In the news this last week, we have seen the kinds of challenges that we face. Federal land management agencies are currently battling severe wildfires in Arizona, which are now coming into New Mexico, Colorado, Alaska, and elsewhere. Obviously we express our concern for the families who have lost their homes, and for those whose property remains at risk. We also want to express our gratitude to the thousands of fire fighters and wildfire managers who are working tirelessly to protect lives, property, and natural resources.

The challenges posed by the larger and more intense drought and wildfires have called for a variety of policy changes to adapt to these new realities. As a result of some of the policies that we have urged here in this committee, for the first time in years, I believe

(1)

the agencies are making progress on a range of critical wildfire management issues. Let me mention five of those.

The FLAME Act established a framework for rational budgeting of emergency wildfire suppression expenses that can help to avoid the enormous disruptions and inefficiencies that frequently have occurred when regular appropriations are insufficient to cover unanticipated emergency costs.

Second, in addition through the FLAME Act, the agencies finally have developed a strong framework for a cohesive wildfire management strategy, and they deserve credit for that.

The agencies are successfully employing collaborative landscape scale projects that reduce fuels and wildfire costs and that improve forest and watershed health.

With the support of the economic stimulus package of a few years ago, the Forest Service reduced wildfire risk by conducting fuel and restoration treatments across a record number of acres during the last 2 years.

Finally, the agencies are fighting fires in a more cost effective manner since adopting a more flexible management response protocol and utilizing state-of-the-art predictive technologies.

Certainly there are significant challenges that remain. Forest health and wildfire management are related areas where I think we need to be careful in our important effort to reduce spending. I fear that we may be headed toward an approach that turns out to be penny wise and pound foolish. For example, the agencies do not have adequate resources to reduce hazardous fuels and restore forest and rangeland health, particularly against a background of growing climate-related vulnerability. Recent cuts to the Forest Service work force are accelerating the problem of a rapidly diminishing force of available critical firefighters. The result is likely to be significantly higher costs to taxpayers and the economy as a result of severe wildfires.

Another challenge that looms large given our fiscal situation is the fact that the Nation's remaining fleet of aging air tankers needs to be replaced or restored in the near future. The cost for doing that will be quite substantial, and it cannot be covered from within the agencies' existing budgets.

I hope our witnesses can help us understand how we can continue to make progress in wildfire management. Let me defer to Senator Murkowski for her comments.

STATEMENT OF HON. LISA MURKOWSKI, U.S. SENATOR FROM ALASKA

Senator MURKOWSKI. Thank you, Mr. Chairman. I appreciate the hearing this morning. Welcome to our colleague, Senator Kyl. I think oftentimes we are brought together by things that are happening in our States. I know that you have been very anxious about the fires in Arizona that are now coming into New Mexico. In Alaska we have got some significant fires burning as well. I am watching the East Volkmar fire very carefully because we have got a family cabin that has been sitting out there. You worry about these things. You worry about what is happening within any given fire season, but to those who have lost property, those who have been threatened, we are very concerned. I know, Senator Kyl, you are quite anxious about what is going on in your State.

But we have to wonder how many times do we have to have a fire season like we are having now before we are really going to collectively work to protect our forests? It was about a decade ago that the Rodeo-Chediski fire consumed 468,000 acres on the Apache-Sitgreaves National Forest. A couple of days later, we had the Biscuit fire that burned nearly 500,000 acres in the Siskiyou National Forest in southern Oregon and northern California. In 2002 three heavy fire fighting aircraft suffered structural failures, which led to the grounding of more than half of the available aircraft that had been used to drop slurry on these fires. The grounding of the aircraft reduced the number of companies that supplied these aircraft, and subsequently the number of aircraft we had available for the slurry dropping duty was down by over 60 percent in 2004.

So, we fast forward to today. Thus far this fire season, we have burned over 4.1 million acres. Today, the Wallow fire in Arizona is burning just 40 miles to the east of where the Rodeo-Chediski fire burned back in 2002. As of yesterday, 430,000 acres had been burned.

Back in 2003, we authorized and funded a prodigious amount of pre-suppression and hazardous fuels work through the Healthy Forest and Forest Restoration programs, but we are just not seeing much as a consequence of that. We have got little to show for it.

Our forests are no more able to withstand the ravages of fire and/or insects than they were 10 years ago. Even after every forest service supervisor signed a pledge to fully implement up to 20 million acres in the Healthy Forest Restoration Act, today less than one-third of the authorized projects have been accomplished. I have to believe that this failure rests with the land management agencies.

In 2003, we asked the Forest Service to answer the question, "what do you need?" What do you need to replace the heavy fire fighting aircraft that were grounded in 2002? It took 10 years to develop the answer, and when it came it was with a $2 billion price tag during a time when Congress is cutting the Federal budget by 15 to 20 percent. It included no recommendations to how we were going to pay for it.

Even more frustrating is that the agency seems to be fixated on one aircraft type and refuses to consider any other alternatives. Last month, Chief Tidwell told me that the Forest Service would work to acquire a variety of aircraft types, but his staff continues to tell people that the agency will only accept an aircraft that can carry 3,000 gallons of slurry. I just do not understand why the Forest Service continues to tell the aircraft manufacturers and others here in Congress that whatever new aircraft it acquires is going to need to carry 3,000 gallons of slurry.

So, my message to the land management agencies is this: develop a procurement plan to replace the aging aircraft that looks at a variety of types of size aircraft; develop the plan so you have got the flexibility to drop slurry, foam gel, or water; develop it to take advantage of the lakes and rivers that hold millions upon millions of gallons of water that could and should be dropped by water scooping aircraft; do not ignore the opportunity to keep the existing fleet operational longer; and finally, aggressively begin to use all of the authorities that this Congress has given you.

I want to see more healthy forest restoration projects. I want to see more large-scale restoration projects and within this decade, not 10 years from now, 20 years from now, 30 years from now, because as I look back on all the lost opportunities of the last 10 years, none pains me more than the failure of our land management agencies to use those authorities that Congress has provided.

Mr. Chairman, I do hope that today we will get some updates, but also perhaps a better understanding as to how the land management agencies can use those authorities that we have given them more effectively.

Thank you.

The CHAIRMAN. Before we hear from our two scheduled witnesses, Senator Kyl wished to address the committee and give us an update on the circumstances that his State has faced, which of course has been catastrophic with this current fire that continues. So, we welcome you, Senator Kyl. Thank you for coming, and please tell us whatever you think the committee needs to know.

STATEMENT OF SENATOR JON KYL, U.S. SENATOR FROM ARIZONA

Senator KYL. Thank you very much, Mr. Chairman, and I very much appreciate both your opening statement and Ranking Member Murkowski's statement. Right on the target. I do want to say that when this hearing is traditionally held about this time of the year about going into the fire season, in your State and mine, of course, fire season starts in May. In our case, it is already well under way.

I would like to ask each of the members of the committee who are here and the staff to please read the statement. It will take about two and a half minutes.

I would rather just talk about what I know from firsthand observations. I want to begin by thanking all of the personnel who have been fighting the fires in Arizona. We now have almost 800,000 acres burning or burned in just four fires so far during this fire season in Arizona. You mentioned the Wallow fire, which is by far the largest; it is in the Arizona White Mountains. The Apache-Sitgreaves Forest just east, as Senator Murkowski said, of the Rodeo-Chediski fire of 9 years ago. Those fires destroy at least— well, in the case of just those two alone, you are going to be at about a million acres of Ponderosa pine, dug for Blue Spruce, and a lot of meadowlands, but an incredibly pretty part of our State of Arizona. There is a booklet that has just a few pictures that you can see.

From the map here of the Wallow fire, you can see with each of the colors how rapidly the fire moved, starting in the extreme southwest part and then moving on up through the others. If I could just go to the map and point out a couple of things, I think it might help.

About 10,000 people had to be evacuated from the town of Eager and Springerville here. The town Nutrioso right here was almost surrounded by the fire. The town of Alpine here literally is surrounded by the fire. The little community of Greer here—Greer got hit the worst, and I will describe that in just a moment. The fire started here and rapidly moved in this direction.

The problem with this fire was the wind. Yes, it is very, very dry. It is warm. But the winds were 40 miles an hour gusting up 60, and you cannot fight fires in those conditions. The big tankers were not usable because they simply couldn't drop the retardant or water on the targets with any degree of precision. So, helicopters were the only option in many situations.

We have a cabin in the community of Greer, and last Friday— a week ago Friday we were having dinner with four—three of our neighbors, and that cabin where we were sitting out on the deck and looking at the beautiful landscape, is now gone, totally destroyed. It is just a half a mile from where our place is. About 22 homes along a half mile stretch of road were lost in that community of Greer. The fire came down over a ridge, and the firefighters had to evacuate very quickly because of the speed with which the fire progressed. They could not stop it.

We have evidence already that the areas that were thinned performed much better than the areas that were not. I believe, and will leave it to Chief Tidwell and the others who will give us the after action report, but I believe they will conclude that the communities of Alpine, Nutrioso, Springerville, and Eager were saved because of thinning in the vicinity of those communities. Of course, the fire burned more slowly in some other areas.

The problem is, as Senator Murkowski pointed out, we are just treating a drop in the bucket when it comes to the amount of acreage that we have to treat. The area of the Apache-Sitgreaves had the biggest contract for Forest Service stewardship to treat 150,000 acres over 10 years. Over the last 7 years, we have treated almost 49,000 acres. That is at a cost of about $2.5 million a year, which includes all of the planning and preparation costs. Clearly, we have a long way to go. The fires are rapidly outstripping our ability to do this on a larger scale.

As a couple of you have alluded to, you do not want to be penny wise and pound foolish, as the chairman said. The costs of fighting the fires and reconstructing afterward far exceed the prevention costs. It is like any other medical situation. Prevention will save you a lot of money in the long run, but it does require an upfront commitment.

But it is not just preventing fires. The management of forests make them more healthy. You have better flora and fauna. The ecology is superior, less prone to disease. Water runoff is better. In all respects, if you can do the treatment early, you are going to save money in the long run.

This one fire—Wallow fire—alone has already cost $65 million. Think about how much land we could have treated if we had put that money up front.

There are photographs in a book that is being passed around to show you just some of what the area looks like. One interesting photograph shows near Alpine, one of the villages saved here, untreated area versus treated area. You all know exactly what happens. In the treated area, the fire lays down and they are better able to control it.

What we have tried to create in Arizona is a new program for larger area treatment. The area that we would be talking about is on a scale of 500,000 to a million or more acres. The proposal on the table is called the Four Forest Restoration Initiative, or Four FRI. It is a collaboration between all of the stakeholders, including the environmental community and all others. It is—the whole concept is we have got to treat large areas or there is not going to be anything left to treat by the time we get around to it.

So, what I am hoping is that the committee can focus on why we are not doing what we need to do. I have some recommendations in my statement. One of them has to do with the costs for the Forest Service associated with the potential cancellation of contracts and the need for front end bonding, which just adds to the cost. That is one thing I think we need to deal with. We also need to obviously commit more resources to do the thinning in advance of the fires rather than trying to pull the money together to fight the fires.

There is so much more I would like to say about this, but if I could just urge my colleagues to read the statement. We are now beginning to look at the costs of reconstruction here, the bare expenses, the other indirect costs of the cleanup and treatment to try to begin to restore.

It is impossible the ecosystem losses. I mean, the Western Forest Leadership Coalition, which is a partnership between State and Federal Government entities, estimate the costs are two to 30 times the reported suppression costs. The Rodeo-Chediski fire that the Senator from Alaska mentioned, the true total cost was estimated to be closer to $308 million; in other words, about 15 times the cost to suppress it. So, you look at what happens after the fire, and the costs in every respect are just devastating.

So, I urge the committee to work up recommendations for what we can do to prevent this kind of destruction. I will certainly pledge my best efforts, not only to support that, but to come up with the resources necessary to accomplish it so that we do not continue to suffer the kind of devastation that is afflicting my State right now.

I thank all of you for your attention.

[The prepared statement of Senator Kyl follows:]

PREPARED STATEMENT OF HON. JON KYL, U.S. SENATOR FROM ARIZONA

Thank you for holding this hearing on wildfire management and for agreeing to give me a few minutes to come talk to you today.

I want to start by first thanking all of the firefighters and other personnel for their service in combatting the wildfires in my state and across the nation. It is not easy. I want them to know I appreciate their tireless efforts.

Arizona is ground zero so far this fire season for mega-fires—those fires that burn tens of thousands of acres—sometimes in just hours.

The Wallow Fire on the Apache-Sitgreaves Forest in the White Mountains of Eastern Arizona has grown to nearly a half a million acres in just 2 weeks charring in its wake some of the most beautiful Ponderosa Pine country in the state. (PHOTOS and MAP) Almost 10,000 people were forced to evacuate. Based on a structural assessment conducted over the weekend, Greer, has been the hardest hit. When the fire rolled in to the community on Wednesday last week it destroyed 22 homes and 24 other buildings out of a total of 50 structures destroyed in the fire to date. The fire is just 18 percent contained as of this morning and has crossed the border into the neighboring state of New Mexico.

This fire, however, is not the only one burning in Arizona, the Horseshoe Fire, the Murphy Complex and the newest, the Monument Fire, have already blackened another 200,000 acres. These are some of the most beautiful grasslands and rugged mountain ranges in southern Arizona (Chiricahua mountains). Given the conditions and the continued fire risk, on June 9, the Coronado National Forest issued an order temporarily closing large parts of the forest to visitors.

In Arizona alone, the fire suppression bill is over $65 million and growing.

It all seems horribly reminiscent of the disastrous fire season of 2002, when 6.9 million acres burned across the West. That year the Rodeo-Chediski Fire, the largest fire in Arizona's history, hit the same forest as the Wallow, in an area just 40 miles northwest, burning over 468,000 acres, including a large portion of the Fort Apache Reservation. Over 490 structures were destroyed, and more than 30,000 residents of nearby communities were evacuated. The Forest Service spent over $47 million to extinguish the blaze. Unfortunately, the Wallow Fire will likely over take the Rodeo-Chediski fire in size and cost before it is extinguished.

The millions of dollars spent year after year on fire suppression do not reflect the true costs of unnaturally severe wildfire. Fire suppression costs are only the immediate costs that are the most easily quantifiable and reported to the public. The affected communities and the ecosystem itself will experience longer-term impacts; the costs of which dwarf the costs of the wildfire but are often difficult to capture. Specifically, these costs include: (1) direct rehabilitation costs/ BEAR expenses (post-fire flooding and soil erosion, property loss recovery), (2) indirect costs (healthcare and mental health treatment costs, loss of life, reduced property values, and lost revenues to residents and businesses) and (3) ecosystem costs (reduced watershed function, air and water quality impairment, loss of wildlife habitat, water infrastructure damage and accelerated carbon release for long-periods post-fire). The Western Forestry Leadership Coalition, a state and federal government partnership, estimates these costs are 2 to 30 times the reported suppression costs.[1] For example, the Rodeo-Chediski Fire's true total cost was closer to $308 million, 15 times the cost to suppress it.[2]

Although the need to suppress fires is not going to go away, it is widely recognized that active forest restoration management can reduce the risk of catastrophic fire, increase firefighting safety and effectiveness, improve recovery time and contribute to ecosystem function, before, during and after a fire. In Arizona we have seen first hand that treatments work. Early reports from the Wallow Fire suggest that, in areas that have been thinned under the White Mountain Stewardship Project, flames dropped to the ground and burned more slowly. For example, in Alpine, one of the communities hit, firefighters told reporters that they were better able to protect it because of the thinning that had been done around the community.[3] Reports indicate the same positive fire behavior was displayed in treated areas near Eager and Nutrioso.[4] Even in Greer, there is a big difference between the areas treated versus areas not treated.[5]

The White Mountain Project is the first large scale Forest Service stewardship contract in the nation. Awarded in 2004, to Future Forest LLC, a local business, the contract had as its goal treating 150,000 acres of the Apache-Sitgreaves Forest over 10 years. Over the last seven years nearly 49,000 acres[6] have been treated at a cost of approximately $2.5 million a year including all planning and prep costs. It has also successfully developed new markets for woody biomass, creating a demand for 15,000 acres per year during one of the most severe economic downturns the wood products industry has seen. Although costs are still relatively high, when compared to the costs of suppression and the indirect costs of catastrophic wildfire, it is a small price to pay. Besides, management of national forest system lands is a federal responsibility. Prevention is always cheaper than fighting the disease.

I would be remiss if I did not point out that the stewardship contracting tool this project utilizes will expire in 2013 if Congress does not act to reauthorize it. Obligating cancellation ceiling reserves for these contracts is also problematic and will likely require a legislative fix.[7]

The current federal system continues to give funding priority to suppression. If we are going to save what is left of our forests we must change our priorities and aggressively treat our forests at the pace and scale these fires are occurring.

---

[1] Western Forestry Leadership Coalition, April 2009, updated April 2010. The True Cost of Wildfire in the Western U.S. at p. 14.

[2] Id. at p. 5.

[3] McKinnon, Shaun. Wallow Fire may be preview of things to come, experts say. The Arizona Republic (June 12, 2011).

[4] Statements from Chris Knopp, Apache-Sitgreaves Forest Supervisor.

[5] Davis, Tony. Thinning likely reduced fire's destructive power. June 12, 2011.

[6] Future Forests LLC. See www.futureforest.info.

[7] Letter to Congresswoman Ann Kirkpatrick from Thomas Vilsack, USDA Secretary dated August 31, 2010.

That means thinking big and acting now. Treatments focused solely on hazardous fuel reduction around communities may be appropriate in some cases, but they do not achieve the enduring fire protection and ecosystem restoration that are urgently required. A greater investment in landscape-scale forest restoration treatments will reverse the degradation of our forests while simultaneously reducing the risk of catastrophic crown fires.

I am talking about thinking on a scale of 500,000 to a million or more acres at a time and doing programmatic environmental reviews at that scale too. That's never been done before but Arizona's ready. We have a proposal on the table. It's called the Four Forest Restoration Initiative (4FRI). The 4FRI is an outgrowth of nearly a decade of collaborative efforts and analyses focused on accelerating forest restoration in northern Arizona. The 4FRI is rooted in the need to accelerate forest restoration and to shift restoration and management efforts from a short term, project-by-project basis to an integrated, landscape-scale program. The goal is to strategically treat about a million acres across four national forests in Northern Arizona over the next 20 years. Bear in mind, that's how many acres burned in just the Wallow fire this year and the Rodeo-Chediski fire 9 years ago.

In order for this effort to be successful it is going to require a significant federal investment including funding and other resources. In addition, industry will need to come to the table to help offset treatment costs. But just as important, it is going to require cooperation from the environmental activist community. Taylor McKinnon from the Center for Biological Diversity stated in a recent opinion piece about such cooperation that, "Our Ponderosa-Pine Forests deserve as much."[8] I agree.

There are things Congress can do to help:

- Reauthorize and make permanent the stewardship contracting tool. Long-term wood supply guarantees are necessary in order to attract private investment to our forests to accomplish the restoration work that needs to be done.
- The Energy Independence and Security Act of 2007, includes a 36 billion-gallon renewable fuels standard (RFS), a portion of which will be made from biomass. A last-minute change in the legislation's definition of renewable biomass, however, prevents almost all federal land biomass such as trees, wood, brush, thinnings, chips and slash from counting toward the mandate if it is used to manufacture biofuels. That makes no sense and we need to change it.
- Support full funding for the implementation of the Southwest Forest Health and Wildfire Prevention Act and the Forest Landscape Restoration Act so that we can get effective science-based restoration on the ground at landscape scales now when it can still make a difference.

Thank you for your time and attention. I look forward to working with my colleagues on these important issues.

The CHAIRMAN. Thank you, Senator Kyl, and we obviously appreciate the great damage that is being done to your State and sympathize with you and all the people of Arizona in that connection.

Why do we not go ahead and dismiss you and invite our two witnesses? Mr. Tom Tidwell, who is chief of the Forest Service, and Ms. Kim Thorsen, who is deputy Assistant Secretary for Law Enforcement, Security, Emergency Management and Wildland Fire in the Department of Interior.

We appreciate both of you being here. Chief Tidwell, did you want to start, and then we will hear from Ms. Thorsen after you are finished. Take whatever time you need to make your main points. Obviously both of your statements will be included in our record.

STATEMENT OF TOM TIDWELL, CHIEF, FOREST SERVICE, DEPARTMENT OF AGRICULTURE

Mr. TIDWELL. Thank you. Mr. Chairman, Ranking Member Murkowski, and members of the committee, I want to thank you for the opportunity to appear before you today.

---

[8] McKinnon, Taylor. Cooperation Crucial to Forest Restoration, Arizona Republic (June 13, 2011).

9

The Forest Service, the Federal agencies, our State, the tribal governments, and our local fire departments, together have the premier wildland firefighting organization in the world. I believe it is an example of government at its best. Together, we continue to be prepared for the 2011 wildland fire season. We have the same level of preparedness that was available last year, including more than 16,000 Federal firefighters with about 70 percent of those from the Forest Service.

So, far the 2011 fire season has been relatively severe. As of today, more than four million acres have burned across the country, which is more than twice the year to date 10-year average. Parts of the south and southwest are in a prolonged drought, and more large fires have burned in the south—most of the large fires have burned in the southeast, Texas, Oklahoma, Arizona, and New Mexico. We also have some large fires in Alaska that the Senator referred to. However, in the Sierras, the Cascades, and the central and northern Rockies, we're having record snow packs. So, it remains to be seen just how severe this fire season is going to be overall.

But based on the level of fire activity and projections for the rest of the year, suppression funding for this year should be sufficient. Appropriations are similar to last year, and we funding from prior years in case of a worse than expected fire season. Together with the FLAME Fund, that should be enough to prevent any transfer of funds from non-fire accounts. Once again, I want to thank you for securing the FLAME account for us.

The FLAME Act also requires that Federal fire managers develop a more cohesive wildland fire management strategy. We wanted to do this in a more collaborative effort than we have done in the past. So, we brought together not only the Federal partners, but our States, the tribes, local and municipal governments to develop a shared national framework.

Now, this cohesive strategy has three main goals. The first is to restore and maintain healthy, resilient landscapes. By vegetation to restore the natural processes and functions, we can minimize the adverse impacts of wildland fire. The second goal is to create fire adapted human communities by reducing fuels in the wildland urban interface, and by helping communities adapt their planning and building practices that make homes and communities safer from wildfire.

We are making progress. Last year, our fuels and forest restoration treatments reduced hazardous fuels on almost three million acres. That is more than twice the area we treated just 10 years ago. With those treatments, we are having success, as these photos show today, the photos that Senator Kyl was referring to. The photo on the left shows severe fire effects in an untreated area on the wall of fire just outside of that community of Alpine. The photo on the right shows an area that was treated under the 10-year White Mountain Stewardship contract.

When the fire hit this treated area, it was a running crown fire up in the top of the trees. It hit the area that was treated. It lost that continuous fuel in the crowns. It dropped down onto the ground, which allowed our firefighters then to be able to get in there and to control it before it burned into the adjacent homes.

Now, the third goal of our fire management strategy is to make safe, effective, risk-based wildfire management decisions. Now, we are going to continue to suppress 98 percent of the fires that we take initial attack on. But to assist with that 2 percent of the fires that become large, we have developed our wildland fire decision support system to help our fire managers make strategic and tactical decisions on these large fires. Public safety, firefighter safety will always be our core agency value.

In closing, I want to touch on the issue with large air tankers. Large air tankers are an effective part of wildland fire suppression. But our current fleet averages more than 50 years old. In the next 10 years, more than half of our large air tankers will need to be replaced, and are studying the options and will be making a recommendation to you by the end of the summer.

I want to thank you, and I look forward to answering your questions.

[The prepared statement of Mr. Tidwell follows:]

PREPARED STATEMENT OF TOM TIDWELL, CHIEF, FOREST SERVICE, DEPARTMENT OF AGRICULTURE

INTRODUCTION

Chairman Bingaman, Ranking Member Murkowski, and members of the Committee, thank you for the opportunity to appear before you today to provide the status of the U.S. Forest Service's wildfire response capabilities.

The Federal Government Agencies responsible for wildland fire fighting are perhaps the premier wildland firefighting organization in the world. Together, we (along with our State, local, and tribal government partners) work to maintain our operational excellence and to continually improve the safety and effectiveness of the fire management program. We take seriously our role in protecting people, property and valuable natural resources from wildfire. We are prepared for the 2011 wildland fire season and are staffed to provide appropriate, risk informed, and effective fire management. We will continue our commitment to aggressive initial attack of wildfires, where appropriate, with full attention to firefighter and public safety. Further, Federal engagement with State and local fire agencies is central to our collective success. Wildfires know no boundaries and we must work within an all-lands context to manage for and respond to wildfires. Our commitment to risk-informed, performance-based strategies will reduce exposure of firefighters and the public at large to unnecessary risk during fire incidents. Additionally, we will continue to provide assistance to communities that have been or may be threatened by wildfire to enable these communities to become more fire resilient and to reduce risks of fire.

NATIONAL COHESIVE WILDLAND FIRE MANAGEMENT STRATEGY

Our commitments—wildfire response, risk-informed performance, support to states and local agencies, and assistance to fire-adapted communities—are consistent with the recently completed National Cohesive Wildland Fire Management Strategy (Cohesive Strategy). The Cohesive Strategy has been embraced by the wildland fire community with statutory authority over wildland fire: federal, tribal, states, counties, municipalities, and local fire departments. The wildland fire community, through the auspices of the Wildland Fire Leadership Council (lead by Secretaries from the Departments of Agriculture, the Interior, and Homeland Security), developed the Cohesive Strategy. The Forest Service and DOI were a catalyst for the nation-wide collaborative effort among wildland fire organizations—land managers, and policy making officials representing federal, state and local governments, tribal interests, and non-governmental organizations. This blueprint provides a common underpinning for all entities with statutory responsibilities for wildfire. Federal, non-federal, and tribal wildland fire management partners are now engaged in ensuing phases where, development of regional assessments and strategies will support completion of a national risk trade-off analysis, due next year.

The three main components of the Cohesive Strategy provides a framework for the wildland fire program as a whole. These components are:

• Restoring and Maintaining Resilient Landscapes

- Creating Fire-Adapted Communities
- Wildfire Response

Restoring and Maintaining Resilient Landscapes

The first component of the Cohesive Strategy involves the restoration of land-scapes to help promote ecosystem health and resiliency. Wildland fire has a valuable natural role in many ecosystems, helping to regulate forest and rangeland composition. We continually strive to safely allow fire to play its natural role in creating resilient landscapes. However, many ecosystems across the country are out of balance and are in need of restoration. This ecological imbalance is manifested by an increased fuel accumulation and infestation by invasive pests and results in ecosystems that are more threatened by wildfire. A high-risk fire environment may result in adverse effects on natural resources and poses great risks for local communities. Added to the effects of climate change, these imbalanced ecosystems often lead to higher fire risk potential, which contribute to extreme fire behavior and severe fire effects, such as significant impacts to municipal water supplies.

By managing vegetation and restoring natural function and the resiliency of the land, we can positively influence fire behavior and minimize the negative impacts of fire. Through a combination of mechanical treatment and managed fire, we can improve the health of some fire-adapted ecosystems and prevent heavy accumulations of highly flammable fuels. In FY 2010, the Forest Service treated over 2 million acres for hazardous fuels reduction, with the majority in the Wildland Urban Interface. This fiscal year, we have already treated over 900,000 acres.

The Integrated Resource Restoration (IRR) line item proposed in the President's FY 2012 budget, applied in conjunction with our hazardous fuels program, will help the agency more efficiently restore ecosystems balance. Combining the existing programs will improve land management professionals ability and flexibility to meet a wider range of ecological, economic and social values than possible under the current structure. This will enable more work to get accomplished on the ground. IRR will allow larger projects to be undertaken through the emphasis on collaboration with stakeholders, internal multi-disciplinary planning, and a well-crafted accountability system.

In addition, the Forest Service will continue to expand community engagement in restoration efforts on National Forest System land through the Collaborative Forest Landscape Restoration (CFLR) Program. In FY 2010, 10 CFLR projects in Idaho, California, Colorado, Arizona, New Mexico, Montana, Washington, Oregon, and Florida were funded by the CFLR Fund. CFLR projects are proposed through multi-stakeholder collaborative planning at a local level, nominated by the Regional Foresters to the Secretary, who takes into consideration recommendations made by an advisory committee.

Creating Fire-Adapted Communities

The second component of the Cohesive Strategy involves working collaboratively with non-governmental organizations as well as federal, state, local and tribal governments to strengthen fire-adapted human communities. An all-lands approach, along with emphasizing individual responsibility, is critical to minimizing risk to communities.

This second component of the Cohesive Strategy relies on coordination and work already taking place among the federal agencies, states, and communities. Community Wildfire Protection Plans (CWPPs) play an important role at the local level in providing specific risk-assessments to a county or community. CWPPs are a comprehensive wildfire planning tool for a community that is supported by the the Federal Government in partnership with State forestry agencies. By providing Federal support to state and local wildland fire agencies, we enhance our capability to work together to create these important plans and bring awareness of shared wildfire risk to communities.

Additional activities include:

- The International Association of Fire Chiefs, with help from the Federal Government, sponsored a forum to identify, share opportunities, and prioritize mitigation needs for a wide range of private sector partners.
- The Fire-Adapted Communities Project gathers all wildland urban interface mitigation tools into one toolbox to assist in the implementation of Community Wildfire Protection Plans by providing communities, organizations, fire departments, and the public with the information they need to reduce their risk of wildfire.
- The Ready, Set, Go! and Firewise projects are part of our Fire-adapted Communities program. With our State, local and NGO partners, we are reaching out

to increase the 600 Firewise communities we have today to over 1,000 communities by 2013. By combining Firewise with the Ready, Set, Go! principles, we are working together to make communities in fire-prone areas more resilient to catastrophic loss.

Wildfire Response

In preparing for the 2011 fire season, the Federal Government worked along with the tribes and the states to ensure we had adequate firefighting resources prepared and positioned. Fire managers will assign local, regional, and federal firefighting personnel and equipment based on anticipated fire starts, actual fire occurrence, fire spread, and severity. All federal, state, and tribal wildland fire agencies are represented in the National Wildfire Coordination Group. This group provides oversight to the National Interagency Coordination Center, located at the National Interagency Fire Center in Boise, Idaho, and oversees coordinated wildland firefighting responses throughout the nation. When fire resources in one geographic area are in short supply, the NWCG helps to prioritize, allocate, and, if necessary, re-allocate the resources. Prioritization ensures firefighting forces are positioned where they are needed most. Fire resources such as personnel, equipment, aircraft, vehicles, and supplies are dispatched and tracked through an integrated national system developed by the Forest Service.

In specified instances, the Department of Defense resources may be available to assist. Assistance also may be available under standing international agreements with Canada, Mexico, Australia, and New Zealand if the Secretary determines that no firefighting resources within the United States are reasonably available.

WILDLAND FIRE PREPAREDNESS

Firefighting Forces

Wildfire responses in the United States involve not only the resources of the Federal Government, but also employees from States, tribal governments, and local governments, contract crews, and emergency/temporary hires. For the 2011 fire season, the available firefighting forces—firefighters, equipment, and aircraft—are comparable to those available in 2010, more than 16,000 firefighters available from the Department of Agriculture and the Department of the Interior with approximately70% coming from the Forest Service. The levels of highly-trained firefighting crews, smokejumpers, Type 1 national interagency incident management teams (the most experienced and skilled teams) available for complex fires or incidents, and Type 2 incident management teams available for geographical or national incidents, also are comparable to those available in 2010. Additionally, the federal wildland fire fighting community work with State and local fire departments, which serve a critical role in our initial attack, and in many cases, extended attack success. The Forest Service uses its authority to provide State Fire Assistance funds to State partners to support State fire management capacity. We could not achieve the successes we have without these key partners.

Aviation

Nationally, the wildland firefighting agencies continue to employ a mix of fixed and rotor wing aircraft. The number of these aircraft may fluctuate depending on contractual and other agreements. Key components of the Forest Service 2011 aviation resources include:

- Up to 19 contracted large air tankers (comprising 90% of all large air tankers);
- 77% of the federal wildland fire response helicopters, including:

  —26 Type 1 heavy helicopters;
  —41 Type 2 medium helicopters on national contracts; and
  —52 Type 3 light helicopters on local or regional contracts;

- 15 Leased Aerial Supervision fixed-wing aircraft;
- Up to 12 Smokejumper aircraft;
- 2 heat detecting infrared aircraft;
- 2 single engine air tanker aircraft (SEATs); and
- 300 call-when-needed helicopters.

The Forest Service maintains a contract for a 100-passenger transport jet to facilitate rapid movement of firefighters during the peak of the fire season. The Forest Service also coordinates closely with the Department of Defense in maintaining eight Modular Airborne Fire Fighting Systems (MAFFS) that can be deployed by Air National Guard and Air Force Reserve C-130 aircraft. The MAFFS program provides surge capability for air tanker support on large fires.

Fire Safety

The Forest Service initiated, and continues to use cutting-edge risk management analyses in our strategic and tactical fire management decisions. We have implemented a Risk Management program that focuses on improving wildfire decisions. This program is enhancing the skill of decision makers by allowing managers to evaluate risk and benefit relative to the overall objective of any given wildfire and reducing the level of uncertainty when determining how to respond to a fire. A critical component of the program is furthering the development of tools to help managers and firefighters make better informed decisions about wildfire response. The Wildland Fire Decision Support System (WFDSS) is an example of a tool that assists fire managers and analysts in making strategic and tactical decisions for fire incidents. WFDSS uses fire behavior modeling, economic principles, and information technology combined with land management plans and spatial analysis of a fire to establish a solid foundation for our professional wildland firefighters to make mindful, risk-informed decisions on wildland response. It continues to be a valuable analysis tool in wildland fire management. Our emphasis on safety is a core value to the agency.

Suppression Funding

Finally, the amount of suppression funding appropriated to the Forest Service Wildland Fire Management Account for FY 2011 is similar to the amount appropriated for FY 2010. In addition, the Forest Service has funding from prior fiscal years to allow us to respond to a worse-than-average fire season. These funds together with the FLAME Fund, established by the FLAME Act of 2009, will minimize the need to transfer funds from non-fire accounts to the Wildland Fire Management Appropriation for fire suppression.

Current Wildland Fire Activity

To date, approximately four million acres across the country have burned this calendar year, predominately in the southeast, Texas, Oklahoma, and Arizona[1]. Early spring months were drier than typical across sections of the south and southwest states. The total number of individual fires across the country is less than the ten-year average, but nearly three times more acres have burned than the ten-year average for this time of year. The State of Texas experienced a higher than normal number of fires and acres burned due to a combination of prolonged drought with dry, windy conditions. Drought is forecast to persist or worsen across the south and southwest parts of the nation. The Interagency Fire Predictive Services group is calling for above normal fire potential through June across this area, including Arizona, New Mexico, western Texas, southern Colorado, and Florida. Above normal significant fire potential is also expected in portions of Alaska and Hawaii.

Arizona Fires Update as of Testimony Submission—June 10, 2011

In response to the large fires burning in Arizona, we have deployed more than 2,500 interagency firefighters to protect lives and property through a joint incident command system, and we are coordinating the resources available at local, state and federal levels. While we have prevented the loss of many homes, and have had no loss of life, we anticipate that the current dry and windy conditions will lead to several difficult days of firefighting ahead of us to prevent additional acreage within the state impacted. We are working with local partners to strategically deploy staff and equipment to minimize the impact on homes and communities within the region. The three large fires in Arizona (e.g., the Wallow fire, Horseshoe 2 fire, Murphy fire) are human caused and are still under investigation.

This concludes my statement. I would be happy to answer any questions that you may have.

The CHAIRMAN. Thank you very much.

Ms. Thorsen, go right ahead.

STATEMENT OF KIM THORSEN, DEPUTY ASSISTANT SECRETARY FOR LAW ENFORCEMENT, SECURITY, AND EMERGENCY MANAGEMENT, DEPARTMENT OF THE INTERIOR

Ms. THORSEN. Thank you, Chairman Bingaman, Ranking Member Murkowski, members of the committee. I appreciate the oppor-

[1] National Interagency Fire Center, National Year-to-Date Report on Fires and Acres Burned by State and Agency, March 21, 2011

tunity to appear before you today to discuss the Department of the Interior's readiness for the 2011 wildland fire season.

I am Kim Thorsen. I am the Deputy Assistant Secretary for Law Enforcement, Security, and Emergency Management at Interior. In this capacity, I provide leadership and oversight to the Department's wildland fire program.

If I may, I would like to submit my full statement for the record and summarize the testimony.

The 2011 fire season began in earnest in late April, early May with the ignition of three wildfires that continue to burn in Georgia and North Carolina. Fire season then moved to the southern area of the United States, strongly impacting the drought stricken States of Oklahoma and Texas, and is now in full swing in the southwestern States.

The drought is forecasted to persist or worsen across much of the southern half of the Nation.

More than 20 percent of the United States is managed by the Department, and together with the Forest Service and our other partners at the State, tribal, and local level, we respond to thousands of wildfires across the country every year. Historically and collectively, we have achieved a high success rate in suppressing fires during the initial attack stage.

So far this calendar, more than 31,000 fires have burned over four million acres.

In Alaska, where the Department has significant land management responsibilities, above normal significant fire potential is forecast for portions of the Yukon and Kenai Peninsula where dead and downed insect killed trees and heavy grass understory exist.

The Department, together with the Forest Service, is working to prevent and reduce the effects of large unwanted fires to preparedness activities like risk assessment, prevention and mitigation efforts, mutual aid agreements, firefighter training, acquisition of equipment and aircraft, and community assistance, and hazardous fuels reduction.

For the 2011 fire season, the Department has been and continues to be prepared. The variable firefighting forces are comparable to those available for the last several years. We will deploy approximately 3,500 firefighters, 135 smoke jumpers, 17 type one crews, 750 engines, more than 200 other pieces of heavy equipment, and over 1,300 support personnel to support those fires.

Where possible, the Department will emphasize the hiring of returning veterans to fill the ranks of its firefighting forces.

Aviation assets for fiscal year 2011 are comparable to prior years as well, with exclusive use contracts in place for two water scooping aircraft, 37 helicopters, and 22 other aircraft, such as smoke jumper and air attack platforms. Nearly 60 single engine air tankers are expected to be available through call when needed contracts.

The Department's commitments are in line with the recently completed phase one of the National Cohesive Wildland Fire Management Strategy. Under the direction of the Wildland Fire Leadership Council, the wildland fire community developed a blueprint to collaborate on achieving a shared vision to "safely and effectively

---

extinguish fire when needed, use fire where allowable, manage our natural resources, and, as a Nation, live with wildland fire."

The phase one blueprint called for restoring and maintaining resilient landscapes, creating fire adapted communities, and wildfire response. During phase two, we will continue to work with our Federal, tribal, State, and local partners to assess wildfire risk, develop regional goals, and create a portfolio of strategic actions and activities.

In phase three, we will bring forth the regional strategies into a national strategy where we will create a national risk tradeoff analysis. This national collaborative effort represents a new strategy, a new path forward, and perhaps a new way of thinking about wildland fire, and may pave the way for national, not just Federal, wildland fire management policy, which is not just comprehensive in its scope, but also consistent, coordinated, and complementary across all jurisdictions.

The Department has made significant improvements in is hazardous fuels prioritization and allocation system to ensure funds are directed to the highest priority projects in the highest priority areas. We developed and issued policy that outlines the hazardous fuels prioritization allocation process, and enhanced our computer systems that identify high priority areas for treatment and high priority projects across the Nation.

The Department will continue to pursue efficiencies and reforms that reduce project costs, increase performance, and ensure the greatest value from invested resources, all while strengthening the accountability and transparency of the way in which taxpayer dollars are being spent.

In summary, the Department of the Interior is prepared to meet the wildland firefighting challenges of today, tomorrow, and beyond. We will strive to maintain customary operational capabilities and continue to improve our integrated approach to wildland fire within the Department.

This concludes my statement. I would be happy to answer any questions.

[The prepared statement of Ms. Thorsen follows:]

PREPARED STATEMENT OF KIM THORSEN, DEPUTY ASSISTANT SECRETARY FOR LAW ENFORCEMENT, SECURITY, AND EMERGENCY MANAGEMENT, DEPARTMENT OF THE INTERIOR

Chairman Bingaman, Ranking Member Murkowski, and members of the Committee, thank you for the opportunity to testify today on Department of the Interior's readiness for the 2011 wildland fire season. The U.S. Department of the Interior (DOI), along with the Forest Service within U.S. Department of Agriculture have been and continue to be prepared for the 2011 wildland fire season.

The 2011 fire season began in earnest in late April / early May, with the ignition of three large wildfires that continue to burn in Georgia and North Carolina. More than twenty percent of the United States (490 million acres) is managed by the bureaus within DOI, with fire management responsibilities that stretch from Florida to Alaska, from Maine to California. Historically and collectively, DOI has achieved a high success rate in suppressing fires during the initial attack stage.

Wildland fire behavior and our response are influenced by complex environmental and social factors as discussed in the 2009 Quadrennial Fire Review (QFR). Such factors include the effects of climate change, cumulative drought effects, continued risk in the Wildland Urban Interface, and escalating emergency response.

Nationally, already this fiscal year, approximately more than 46,000 fires have burned more than 4.5 million acres (this calendar year, approximately more than 31,000 fires have burned over 4 million acres), predominantly in the southeast

16

(Texas and Oklahoma) and now the southwest (Arizona and New Mexico) on federal and non-federal lands. Drought is forecast to persist or worsen across much of the southern half of the nation. And in Alaska, where the Department has significant land management responsibilities, above normal significant fire potential is forecast for portions of the Upper Yukon and Kenai Peninsula where dead and down insect-killed trees and heavy grass understory exist.

For the 2011 fire season, available firefighting forces within the Department of the Interior—firefighters, equipment, and aircraft—are comparable to those available for the last several years. Among its bureaus, the Department will deploy approximately 3,500 firefighters, 135 smokejumpers, 17 Type-1 crews, 750 engines more than 200 other pieces of heavy equipment (dozers, tenders, etc.) and about 1,300 support personnel (dispatchers, fire cache, etc) ; for a total of nearly 5,000 personnel. Where possible, the Department will emphasize the hiring of returning veterans to fill the ranks of its firefighting forces.

Aviation assets for FY 2011 are comparable to prior years as well, with exclusive use contracts in place for 2 water scooping aircraft, 37 helicopters, and 22 other aircraft (smokejumper, air attack, etc.) Nearly 60 single-engine air tankers (SEATs) are expected to be available through call-when-needed contracts.

The federal government wildland fire agencies are working with tribal, state, and local government partners to prevent and reduce the effects of large, unwanted fires through preparedness activities like risk assessment, prevention and mitigation efforts, mutual aid agreements, firefighter training, acquisition of equipment and aircraft, and dispatching; community assistance and hazardous fuels reduction.

All these commitments are in line with the recently completed Phase I of the National Cohesive Wildland Fire Management Strategy. The wildland fire community, under the direction of the Wildland Fire Leadership Council (lead by Secretaries from the Departments of Agriculture, Interior, and Homeland Security), has developed a blueprint for all entities with statutory responsibilities for wildfire to collaborate on achieving a shared vision to "safely and effectively extinguish fire, when needed; use fire where allowable, manage our natural resources, and as a nation, live with wildland fire". The blueprint called for: restoring and maintaining resilient landscapes, creating fire adapted communities, and wildfire response. In addition, the federal government is continuing to work with our non-federal partners to complete Phase II of the Cohesive Strategy this fiscal year, which will develop regional goals and portfolios of actions and activities. Phase III would be a national risk trade-off analysis. This national collaborative effort represents a new strategy, a new path forward and perhaps, a new way of thinking about wildland fire and may pave the way for national, not just federal, wildland fire management policy which is not just comprehensive in its scope, but also consistent, coordinated and complementary across all jurisdictions.

Until then, DOI continues to take full advantage of the current Implementation Guidelines for the Federal Wildland Fire Management Policy. Our unwavering commitment to firefighter and public safety in managing wildfire is the foundation of the fire management program within each DOI bureau. We will continue to respond quickly and effectively to control unwanted wildland fires. Initial action on human-caused wildfire will continue to suppress the fire at the lowest risk to firefighter and public safety. When appropriate, we will also allow fire managers to manage a fire for multiple objectives and increase managers' flexibility to respond to changing incident conditions and firefighting capability, while strengthening strategic and tactical decision implementation supporting public safety and resource management objectives. Our actions will be supported by the Wildland Fire Decision Support System (WFDSS) and our enhanced ability to analyze fire conditions and develop risk informed strategies and tactics, resulting in reduced exposure to unnecessary risk during fire incidents.

The President's Fiscal Year 2012 Budget reflects the commitment of the Administration to implement program reforms to ensure fire management resources are focused where they will do the most good. The 2012 budget proposes a total of $821.5 million to support the fire preparedness, suppression, fuels reduction, and burned area rehabilitation needs of DOI. The 2012 budget request fully funds the inflation-adjusted 10-year average of suppression expenditures of $362.6 million, with the funding split between $270.6 million in the regular suppression account and $92.0 million in the FLAME Fund. Consistent with the FLAME Act, the regular suppression account will fund the initial attack and predictable firefighting costs, while the FLAME Fund will fund the costs of the largest, most complex fires and also serve as a reserve when funds available in the regular suppression account are exhausted.

The President's FY 2012 Budget provides DOI sufficient funding to fully cover anticipated preparedness and suppression needs. The Budget also recognizes the need to invest not just in firefighting related activities, but in hazardous fuels reduction

17

and community assistance, and rehabilitation of burned areas as well. The budget for the Hazardous Fuels Reduction program focuses the program on projects in or adjacent to the wildland-urban interface and the Department has made significant improvements to its Hazardous Fuels Prioritization and Allocation System to ensure funds are directed to the highest priority projects in the highest priority areas. DOI developed and issued policy that outlines the Hazardous Fuels Prioritization and Allocation Process and has enhanced the commuter systems that identify high priority areas for treatment and high priority projects across the nation. We have also worked collaboratively to improve the decision and documentation process. In fiscal year 2011, the bureaus within the Department have funded high priority projects in high priority areas which will result in the mitigation of risks to communities and their values. The Department will continue to pursue efficiencies and reforms that reduce project cost, increase performance, ensure the greatest value from invested resources, all while strengthening the accountability and transparency of the way in which taxpayer dollars are being spent.

In summary, the Department of the Interior is prepared to meet the wildland firefighting challenges of today and tomorrow. DOI will maintain customary operational capabilities and continue to improve the effectiveness and efficiency of the fire management programs. These efforts are coupled with other strategic efforts and operational protocols to improved oversight and use of the latest research and technology to ensure fire management resources are appropriately focused. Specifically, these actions include:

- Continued reduction of hazardous fuels on priority lands in wildland-urban interface areas with its hazardous fuels reduction funds that present the greatest opportunity to reduce the risk of severe damaging fires in the future;
- Continued improvement of decision-making on wildland fires by leveraging the Wildland Fire Decision Support System capabilities to predict what may happen during a fire to safeguard lives, protect communities and enhance natural resources ecosystem health;
- Continued enhancement to wildfire response and efficiency that comes from use of national shared resources, pre-positioning of firefighting resources, and improvements in aviation management;
- Continued review of fire incidents to apply lessons learned and best practices to policy and operations; and
- Continued strategic planning in collaboration with the Forest Service and our state, tribal, and local government to develop meaningful performance measures and implementation plans to address the challenges posed by wildfires in the nation.

Although the Department of the Interior and the Department of Agriculture (USDA) are offering separate written statements today, please be assured that the Departments work collaboratively in all aspects of wildland fire, along with our other federal, tribal, state and local partners. Our statements have been coordinated to ensure a well rounded presentation of our collective fire management program, the common challenges that we face, and our recent efforts to effectively meet these challenges. The two Departments collaborate in the Federal Fire Policy Council, and met just last week to explore some of the issues that are faced by senior executives during periods of significant wildfire activity and to reaffirm their mutual understanding of roles and responsibilities and develop appropriate response scenarios prior to any national emergencies.

Together, we are staffed to provide safe and effective fire management with available firefighting forces—firefighters, equipment, and aircraft. And at the same time, we continue to improve effectiveness, cost efficiency, safety, and community and resource protection in concert with each other.

This concludes my statement. Thank you for your interest in the Wildland Fire Program and the opportunity to testify before this Committee. I welcome any questions you may have and appreciate your continued support.

The CHAIRMAN. Thank you both very much.

Chief Tidwell, let me ask you first. I think you somewhat answered this in your opening statement, but as we look at the situation in my State and around the country, we have got more and more fires starting up. We have a fire reported today that started yesterday at Carlsbad Caverns National Park. We have a fire up around Raton, which has caused the closing of I–25 going between Albuquerque and Denver. In addition, of course, Senator Kyl referred to the fact that the Wallow fire out of Arizona is now coming over and threatening the town of Luna, New Mexico.

What I understood you to say was that you believe the Forest Service has the resources necessary to respond to these fires and the others going on around the country. Is that an accurate understanding of your view?

Mr. TIDWELL. Yes. With the resources that all of the partners bring to the wildland firefighting mission, we believe that we have adequate resources to deal with the fires that we have on the landscape today, with an anticipation of new starts every day.

I want to stress that we always hold resources in reserve to deal with initial attacks so that we always have resources to be able to put on those to stop these new fires from becoming large. But with everything that we have on—that is burning today, plus what we anticipate over at least in the south for another 60 to 45 days, we believe we have adequate resources.

The CHAIRMAN. Thank you. Last year, the Inspector General issued a report that said that regarding the firefighting work force, it concluded that the Forest Service's firefighter work force is shrinking at the same time as its need for qualified firefighters and emergency response managers is increasing. The Inspector General said that insufficient planning could both increase the Forest Service's already significant fire suppression expenditures through the higher costs of using non-Forest Service employees and jeopardize the response capabilities of both the Forest Service and the assisting agencies. Could you give us a little explanation as to how you are responding to that report from the Inspector General?

Mr. TIDWELL. We share the concerns from the Inspector General that we need to ensure that we have a firefighter force in the future. That includes not only the firefighters, but also the overhead positions, the incident commanders that we need to be able to carry out, you know, this mission in the future.

So, I have tasked my team to be looking at some of the things that we can do differently to ensure that we are able to recruit future firefighters and, at the same time, to look at ways that we can accelerate some of the training. Many of our incident commanders, they take over 20 years to be able to acquire the level of experience and training that they need to be an incident commander. So, one of the things that we wanted to look are training requirements and see how we can accelerate that maybe with additional training assignments, and at the same time, to ensure they have the expertise. But that we want to make sure that we have that command system in place, the personnel for the command system, into the future.

The CHAIRMAN. The large fires that we are seeing, this Wallow fire being one example, remind us of why a landscape scale approach to fuel reduction and forest restoration is important. Could you tell us how you think this new collaborative forest landscape restoration program is going, and whether you think that is going to be an effective approach in reducing the risk and the costs of these severe wildfires?

Mr. TIDWELL. Mr. Chairman, I want to thank you for your leadership to provide us with that authority. That is, I believe, the model for the future, where we can bring people together from all interests to look at these much larger areas than we ever have before. In the case with the these projects, there are over 50,000 acres. Then to also provide a commitment for long-term funding, not just a 1-year commitment of funds. This will allow us to be able to look at these much larger landscapes, ideally do environmental analysis for much larger areas, thus reducing our planting costs, and be able to actually treat enough acres on the landscape where it makes a difference.

Senator Kyl mentioned that in Arizona, where the White Mountain stewardship project, we have been able to treat over 40,000 acres out of the 150,000 that we had hoped to treat during the 10-years. Those projects, as I pointed out in the picture, made the difference in those communities. It is a difference from just losing a few homes to losing all of those homes.

That is the type of work that we need to do, but we need to do it on a much larger scale. I think the Collaborative Force Landscape Restoration projects are definitely the model as we move forward, and it is something we want to continue to expand on.

We did ask for full funding both in fiscal year 2011 and also in fiscal year 2012. We appreciate the support from Congress for the funding we received in 2011. I would really encourage full funding for those projects next year.

The CHAIRMAN. Thank you very much.

Senator Murkowski.

Senator MURKOWSKI. Thank you very much, Mr. Chairman.

Chief, Senator Kyl, in speaking of the Arizona fires, talked about the costs that are associated with it. I think we all recognize that just the dollars that are out there are really quite considerable.

It is my understanding that the East Volkmar fire, which we have been following, has surpassed that $5 million range. It is estimated at about $8 million. By the time everything is contained, I think Senator Kyl mentioned, it will be over $40 million for the Wallow Creek and the others there.

Back in 2009, during the 2009 edition of Wildland Fire, a team of scientists said that the total short-term and long-term costs plus loss attributed to wildfire typically attains amounts that are 10 to 50 times or more reported suppression expenses. Do you agree with that? I mean, when we are talking about the costs of these fires, are we being comprehensive and inclusive in understanding it? Have we really been able to identify what the costs associated with these wildland fires are?

Mr. TIDWELL. Yes, Senator. You know, we have not reviewed those exact figures, but without any question, the true costs, the total costs, of these large wildland fires goes way beyond the suppression costs. Just with the fires we are seeing in Arizona, the emergency rehabilitation that we will need to do, it could easily match the total suppression costs by itself. When you factor in the loss of the resources, the impact to the livestock operators, even though it may only be for a year or so, plus the other damages to fences, there is just no question that those total costs go way beyond the suppression costs.

Senator MURKOWSKI. Does your agency do that calculation, above and beyond the suppression costs? Because we can identify those.

But do you in fact complete a total cost study of a whole season's worth of fires?

Mr. TIDWELL. We have not done that in the past.

Senator MURKOWSKI. Can you do that?

Mr. TIDWELL. It is something I would like to visit with you to see—if some of the information that we already have in our modeling that we use in our decision support system, that may provide you the answer that you are looking for. So, I would like to visit with you on that.

Senator MURKOWSKI. I would like to do that, and I look forward to that.

Let me ask you about the Alaska fire crew recruitment and the issues that are associated with that. We have had this conversation before where we have teams of Alaskans—native fire crews that are standing by the ready to go out and work on the fires. It is always a debate as to who we bring in. We are told that part of the reason that we do not use the local teams is they lack the qualifications needed to serve on the Federal fires. This is something that my constituents are bringing up with me repeatedly. They are saying, "OK, if we do not have the training, why not provide that training so that you do not have that expense of bringing folks up from the lower 48?

On my trip back home this weekend and the weekend before, I sat next to a firefighter from Oregon, and then a firefighter from California who were on their way up. I welcome them. We need the help. But I also want to know what is it that we can do to ensure that the Alaskan native crews actually get out on a job. This is their part of the country. They know and understand it well. What do we need to be doing better?

Mr. TIDWELL. Senator, the Alaskan native crews are handled through the Department of Interior, but I will say that ideally we would like to have those crews that are trained locally. It is more cost effective to be able to have those folks there, and at the same time then after the Alaska fire season is over, we often then bring those crews down into the lower 48, where they will often spend another month or two before they get to go back home.

Senator MURKOWSKI. All right.

Mr. TIDWELL. So, it takes a combination of both. It is why we are so successful in the way that we all work together, and that these firefighting resources are mobile. And there may be times that we do need to bring personnel up to Alaska, but we always try to reach out and train local crews so they are there. They are available, and so we do not have to wait for them to be transported.

Senator MURKOWSKI. We are looking also to the cost of it.

Mr. TIDWELL. Yes.

Senator MURKOWSKI. It takes a lot to move these men and women back and forth. If we have got the locally trained crews and they are good, which they are; we have got some great hot shot crews up there—that is one way that we can be looking at the cost side of this.

I hope we are going to have an opportunity for a second round, Mr. Chairman, because I have got a lot more questions here. Thank you.

The CHAIRMAN. Thank you.

Senator Wyden.

Senator WYDEN. Thank you, Mr. Chairman.

Chief, all the senators are saying—those from the west—that our forests are just taking a beating because of insufficient thinning. It is obvious that these overstocked stands are just magnets for, you know, disease and insects, and when they are dry, they just go up in smoke. Every time you all come on up here, you talk to us, particularly when we highlight some of the innovative approaches that we are seeing around the country. Like on the east side of Oregon, you all said we have got to have more money. We have got to have more money.

We went and looked at your fiscal year 2012 budget justification. You proposed rescinding close to $200 million from the fiscal year 2011 budget, and on page 11–14 of the budget justification, you proposed more reductions in the hazardous fuels budget.

So, I am trying to reconcile these two statements, the one that you need more money and, second, actually what is in the budget. So, why do you not tell me how those two are consistent to start with?

Mr. TIDWELL. Senator, with our fiscal year 2011 funding, especially for hazardous fuels, it is basically the same as we had in fiscal year 2010. In fiscal year 2012, there is a slight reduction. But the big change in our proposal for fiscal year 2012 is this concept of having an integrated resource restoration budget line item. We want to focus our hazardous fuel funding on the wildland urban interface, and then we want to take some of that fuels funding and put it into the integrated resource restoration so that in the landscapes—the forests that are outside the wildland urban interface, we can take this much more integrated approach to be able to not only address the need to reduce that hazardous fuel through thinning, but also accomplish the watershed improvement work, the wildlife habitat improvement work. By putting those funds together, we feel that we will increase our effectiveness, and at the same, not ask for more funding.

Senator WYDEN. I just have to tell you, I think this is still, as it relates to the budget, kind of funny money. I mean, you all talk to us about the integrated resources program, like that. You talk to us about the collaborative forestry program like that. We have essentially got one out of our nine, you know, forests. Every year, the problem just grows and grows. My own sense is I think if you do not deal with these reductions—you have said they are small; we do not see them as small—in the hazardous fuels program, this problem is just going to continue, you know, to grow. We are going to continue to bring it up. When it is dry, we are going to see these infernos. That is what these fires are in dry areas. They are not natural fires; they are infernos.

So, let me ask you about one other point, and that is the Wildland Fire Aviation Program. This, as you know, has been under the microscope for what seems like, you know, eons. It is a fleet that is aging rapidly. Somehow, getting an adequate plan for the future just is not coming together. I mean, this has been almost the longest-running battle since the Trojan War to get you all to update this fleet. It was reported again in the papers. Why is it taking so long to get an adequate replacement fleet, and particularly, a plan so that we will know for certain when this is going to happen?

Mr. TIDWELL. Senator, as I mentioned earlier, we will be bringing our plan up here, you know, by the end of this summer. Some of the things that is taking the time is that we wanted to make sure that we had the information that we needed. We worked—in fact, the Department of Defense just completed a study that you requested for us to take a look at being able to use military aircraft on a full time purpose for wildland firefighting. They have completed their report. We are also still waiting for the report that the RAND Corporation has promised us in July that would look at what is the right mix between large air tankers, small air tankers, scoopers, et cetera?

So, we have been gathering information, but at the same time, continuing to work with our contractors that have done a very good job to be able to maintain the existing fleet so that we can still respond where we need large air tankers.

Senator WYDEN. Can you give me your sense of a target date when the agency would have an adequate replacement fleet? I mean, just give us a ballpark when we could expect that fleet to be available to deal with the kind of emergencies that you know creates such a demand?

Mr. TIDWELL. What I envision is that we are going to be looking at every option that is available today and to be able to lay out a strategy that will continue to maintain an adequate fleet. We have an adequate fleet today. We want to make sure that we have that 10 years from now, 20 years from now. So, our recommendation will include a strategy that will allow us to work forward, and at the same time to work with our contractors to find ways to ensure that we will have that adequate fleet into the future.

Senator WYDEN. My time is up. I can just tell you, everybody remembers those two air tanker crashes that took the lives of pilots and maintenance personnel in 2002. I do not share your view that things, with respect to today's situation, are adequate. I think the government has got to do a lot better, and I hope we will accelerate the efforts.

Thank you, Mr. Chairman.

The CHAIRMAN. Senator Lee.

Senator LEE. Thank you, Mr. Chairman.

Mr. Tidwell, I understand that new fire management policies are in place, and that sometimes when implementing these policies, it results in longer-burning fires at times that can adversely affect neighboring jurisdictions. What are you doing to work with local officials to resolve any conflicts that might develop as this happens?

Mr. TIDWELL. Senator, when a fire starts, and especially fires in the back country, we look at the opportunities to be able to manage those firs for some resource benefits if we have the right conditions and we have done the pre-planning.

The first part of that, though, is to be able to sit down with the local jurisdictions, the local communities, and be able to talk through the strategies so that they have an understanding of what we are proposing. We want to be able to work together to be able to take those—use those opportunities, to actually use fire to help reduce some of fuel loading, and actually restore these systems.

23

It is essential we do that together, and that is one of the first things that is done. Even at the start of the season, we want to sit down with our local communities to be able to explain what we would like to do if we get a start under these conditions and be able to talk about it with them and answer their concerns.

Senator LEE. Thank you. On the issue of thinning and making our forests less vulnerable to fires, is there anything that can be done by way of allowing more selective harvesting of lumber in some of those areas to thin that out, and thereby reduce the risk of loss to fire?

Mr. TIDWELL. That is the key to our restoration work. It is the key to our wildland urban interface work is to be able to, as you saw in this one photo. We have numerous pictures around the country of this. Arizona is not the first place that we have seen this. By getting in there and thinning out these stands, it changes the fire behavior dramatically to the point where the fire will get out of the tops of the trees, get down onto the ground where our suppression efforts are then effective.

The level of thinning is dependent on the conditions we have, the slope, how close the homes are, and also the vegetation types.

Senator LEE. Thank you. Ms. Thorsen, cheatgrass is a problem throughout a lot of the west, including my State of Utah. How much of a problem do you think cheatgrass plays in paring your efforts toward fire prevention and in making fires worse when they break out?

Ms. THORSEN. Senator, it is definitely part of the issue that we are facing when it comes to fire activity in the west. One of the things that we have got to help us in that arena is our hazardous fuels prioritization and allocation system, which will help us identify hazardous fuels dollars in areas that are high priority areas and high priority targets.

Now, many of those are in the Woowie area, but we also funds throughout our bureaus that allow us to address a little bit of what the chief said. Habitat restoration so far is outside the Woowie or immediately adjacent to the Woowie. So, we have got some things that we are working on within the Department to address the very issue you are talking about.

Senator LEE. OK. Thank you. Thank you, Chairman.

The CHAIRMAN. Senator Franken.

Senator FRANKEN. Thank you, Mr. Chairman. Chief Tidwell, good to see you again.

The chairman mentioned earlier that climate change is one factor contributing to the fires that we are seeing. Can you comment on that, and on the impacts you think climate change will have on forest fires in the future?

Mr. TIDWELL. Yes, Senator. You know, what we are seeing today in Arizona and other parts of the south is an example of what our scientists say are the effects of climate change. Throughout the country, we are seeing longer fire seasons, and we are seeing snow packs on an average actually disappear a little earlier every spring. So, we have a longer fire season. Like the chairman pointed out, that with this change in climate, we are seeing a much increased frequency of disturbance events, such as drought. Not only are the droughts more frequent, they are also longer in length.

So, in many parts of the west especially, we have seen our fire seasons increase more than 30 days from what we saw in the past. Our scientists believe this is contributed to the change in the climate.

These large fires that we are seeing today, and we have had large fires in the past, but I will tell you, when I was out in Arizona last weekend, and I flew over the Wallow fire, and then stopped to talk to our crews, I have seen a lot of large fires in my career. But I tell you, when I flew up along the west side of that fire and saw about a 30-mile front of active fire on just one side of that, it definitely topped anything that I have seen before.

This is a product of just the prolonged drought, very high, hot, dry conditions, and, of course the winds that Senator Kyl referred to.

We need to do treatments on the land to be able to ensure our communities are safe. We need to do treatments to restore the resiliency, to be able to—so our forests can recover from these fires. But we are going to continue to have large fires, and the changing climate is one of the factors that will contribute to that.

Senator FRANKEN. I would just like to underscore that for members of our body who when we have discussions about the impact of climate, and we are talking about the cost of this. That is a lot of what we are talking about here today is the cost of this.

Sometimes when we talk about energy and we talk about the amount of carbon dioxide that goes into our atmosphere, and we talk about cost, I think that it would be really good for members to take into account this kind of cost. This is a real cost. We are talking about real dollars here. A lot of the focus of this hearing today has been the costs of this. I think that it would be all well and good for members to understand this is related to climate change and how important it is for us to address this and for our—take national action to reduce our carbon emissions.

Now, to that end, we are talking a lot about treating forests. I would like to ask about the opportunity that is sustainable, the harvest of forest biomass offers in enhancing both forest health and in providing a renewable resource for heating and cooling or power production, all three. How are you incorporating the sustainable harvesting of woody biomass in the Forest Service fire prevention plans, and using it to do the kind of—we do in Minnesota, which is use biomass to do, you know, district energy and do heating and cooling and using that to produce energy?

Mr. TIDWELL. Senator, one of the things that we need to continue to do in this country is to maintain our integrated wood products industry, so that the biomass that needs to be removed from these landscapes, that we can put it to beneficial use. Whether it is the sawlogs that need—sawlog diameter trees that need to be removed or the smaller diameter material that could be used for other products, or for biomass production—utilization to produce energy, we need to make sure that we are in—finding ways to build that infrastructure, and especially with the smaller diameter material.

We have the option to either pile it up—pay somebody to pile it up and burn it out there in the woods or we can we can find a way that we can transport it to a facility and be able to convert it into energy. I think that is a much better solution. So, we are going to continue to ask for funding in our biomass grant so that we can encourage this type of infrastructure development around the country, all over the country. It is not the solution, but it is just part of the solution. To me, it just makes better sense than piling this stuff up and burning it.

Senator FRANKEN. Thank you. It seems like a win-win to me.

Thank you, Mr. Chairman.

The CHAIRMAN. Thank you.

Senator Heller.

Senator HELLER. Thank you, Mr. Chairman, and thanks for holding this hearing. I apologize for my tardiness, but this is an important issue to most of us, especially western States, as we deal with these wildfires. I have got a son who attends the University of Southern California, and he is an engineering student. In the summer, Dad makes him fight fires. So, he is currently in Arizona fighting these fires, and he has been there for almost 2 weeks now. I think after 2 weeks, they pull them out, but he has been there at least—more than 10 days. Mom makes him call home every night to make sure that the 21-year-old son is safe.

The CHAIRMAN. Tell him to keep that fire out of New Mexico, would you please?

Senator HELLER. Actually, I told Senator Kyl he was assigned to his house, and that is why it burned the house around him, not his particular residence.

Needless to say, I have seen fuel treatments in the Lake Tahoe Basin and seen this picture. It is exactly the occurrence when correct fuel treatments have been applied. The problem is it is very expensive, and we spend literally hundreds of millions of dollars with these fuel treatments, just in one basin. So, I cannot imagine how expensive that has to be try to do that on a much larger scale. But clearly, the actions and the efforts do work.

One of the problems, of course, we have in Nevada is that 85 percent of the State is owned by the Federal Government, and so what I concern myself is readiness of the Federal Government for some of these wildfires. I have had an opportunity to look at some of the Interior reports, and the outlook on the fire season, and the funding. I guess my concern, since I do have a son that is out there fighting these fires on behalf of the Bureau of Land Management and the efforts, of course, for the residents in Arizona, is if you have sufficient funding. I apologize again for my tardiness, but maybe you have already covered this question, but your physical readiness. If the funding is there, is the physical—and I am talking individuals, enough firefighters, enough equipment, the trucks, the planes, and everything. Do you feel prepared for this wildfire season?

Mr. TIDWELL. Senator, yes. We continue to be prepared this year. We have the adequate resources. I want to just assure you that I will speak for all of the agencies, that we would not allow your son or any other firefighter to go out unless they had the equipment and they had the training and they had passed our physical requirements to ensure that not only can they accomplish their mission to help suppress that fire, but they come home safely.

Senator HELLER. I believe that. I am sure that is that case. I have no reason to believe otherwise.

I want to touch on one other topic quickly that I think is of concern, at least in the State of Nevada and the west as a whole, and that is the threat of these Endangered Species Act listing the sage grouse. When you have a wildfire like this, the impact that that has on the ecosystem, and the competition that you have between wildlife, such as sage grouse, elk, deer, and, for that matter, nonenative species, like wild horses.

If the bird gets listed and you have these fires, I think it will have a devastating impact when you try to balance between the act itself, the wildfires, and the competition that you have between these animals.

Does the BLM have any plans to invest more heavily into pretreatment in these areas when you have this kind of competition going on between the Act itself, between the fires, and between the animals competing for those specific grounds? Is there anything in—that you are doing that would give any priority to treatment in those threatened areas?

Ms. THORSEN. Yes, Senator. The BLM is working very hard in trying to keep it off the endangered species list through hazardous fields treatments and their programs within the Bureau. So, it is a high priority for them. They have other things that they certainly need to balance, but it is absolutely on the list of their high priority items to ensure that that does not happen, for the very reasons that you talk about.

Senator HELLER. Thank you, Mr. Chairman.

The CHAIRMAN. Thank you. Senator Risch.

Senator RISCH. Thank you, Mr. Chairman. Tom, good to see you. Thank you for what you do, and we in Idaho are certainly happy you are where you are, and you have been very helpful to us when we have had issues with the Forest Service.

I guess I come at this a little bit different than a lot of the people here. I think as I look around the room, probably you and I are the only ones with degrees in forest management. Maybe there is a handful of others in here, and probably not many of us, included, I am sure, Senator Franklin—or Senator Franken—have operated a Pulaski on a fighter line before. But when you do that, you get a different perspective, I think, than kind of theoretical approach to fire management and what have you.

By the way, as far as climate change, we had a change in Idaho this year. We got record snow pack. We are probably not going to have much of a fire season, thank goodness. I have got watersheds that 1,000 times—that have 1,000 percent—excuse me—1,000 percent of the average, and it is just stunning the amount of snow that we have this year. So, our concern is probably going to be fire rather—or flood rather than fire.

I appreciate the fine line you guys walk. It just amazes me when I hear people talk about climate change, with all due respect to Senator Franken. Generally, the people who talk about climate change and wring their hands about the fires are the exact same people who when you in the Forest Service tried to remove fuel from a particular watershed are the first ones that file suit to stop from removing that fuel. As all know, over the years—and when I am talking years, I am talking centuries—the original policy of the U.S. Government to do fire control after the big burn in 2009 and

2010 is what we are paying the price for now because the objective was to fight fires, all fires, and suppress them at all times and all places.

So, that went along for a lot of years. We did a good job of suppressing fires. We never had a big burn again. Then over the years, the Federal Government has also had a policy, not through the government, but through the courts, to stop taking the fiber out of the forest. The result of that is we got today, which are catastrophic fires. As you know in Idaho, we have really suffered from that over the last decade.

So, I appreciate the fine line that you walk and the difficulties that you have. We had, as I think you know, when I started in the State legislature in 1975, we had 42 operating mills in southern Idaho. Today we have two. One of them was built was built with stimulus money, so it's a Federal Government financed mill and not there because of the free market forces that should be operating. So, since we are down to these two mills, it is very difficult to remove fiber from the forest.

So, again, I appreciate what you do. I appreciate the fine line you have to talk. I hope you will continue to educate people about how important it is to remove fuel. Removing fuel is so important when it comes to fire control, particularly in forests that are thriving and the ones that do produce the board feet that we could use.

It is a difficult task. I know most people do not have the technical understanding of how acres vary from acre to acre of the difference and the amount of fuels on the ground. It is a great picture that you have provided here. I think you and I have probably seen—have seen examples of this all over. As you know, when you are out on a fire, you get the old maps out, you know, hope it hits one that is burned within the last 5 or 10 years because that, of course, changes the dynamics of the fire entirely.

The unfortunate thing about just plain fuel treatment is how economically inefficient that it is. Again, if it was turned over to the private sector to be able to remove it, to be able to use it, to saw it, to use it for bio fuels or whatever, it would certainly help us at the Federal level as far as the dollars and cents we spend doing this.

So, thank you for what you do. We have, as you know, NIFC, national Fire Center, in Boise. The guys are probably going to be doing most of the work outside of Idaho this year, which is a good thing. It is our turn to not have the fires.

Thank you for what you do.

Thank you, Mr. Chairman.

The CHAIRMAN. Thank you. Let me ask another question.

The FLAME Act, which you have referred to and which I have referred to, passed in the last Congress and it requires the agencies to periodically submit predictive estimates for wildfire suppression costs so that Congress is adequately informed of the fiscal situation as it is working on appropriations bills. To date, neither of the departments, Agriculture or Interior, have submitted those reports within the timeframes required by the Act. Obviously it is sort of a waste of the effort and resources to develop the reports if they are going to be obsolete by the time we get to see them. So, getting these reports cleared and submitted in a timely manner will be critical if we are going to be able to help avoid the fire borrowing situation we used to find ourselves in.

So I would urge both of you to just take a message back to your respective departments that we need to come up with some way to get that information to the Congress in a timely way so we can act upon it. I do not know if either of you have any comments on that. I am not really asking you to respond. I think, as I understand it, the problem is not getting the reports done, but getting them cleared. Is that an accurate understanding?

Mr. TIDWELL. Senator, first of all, you know, I agree with you, and I apologize that we have not sent those reports out. It is information that we use. It is essential that we share that so that you can factor that into your decisionmaking. You have my assurance that in the future we will make sure that we have those up here.

If it takes a little more time to get them through our clearance process, we are going to do that to make sure you have that. I am hoping that we will have them up here this week.

The CHAIRMAN. That will be very helpful.

Ms. Thorsen, did you have any comments?

Ms. THORSEN. Senator, yes. The Department of the Interior did submit a report dated April 27 to the Hill. So, we will get you a copy of that——

The CHAIRMAN. OK.

Ms. THORSEN [continuing]. So you have that. Then our May report is in process, so we are starting the process, and we will be sure to get it here on time.

The CHAIRMAN. OK. Thank you very much.

Senator MURKOWSKI. Thank you, Mr. Chairman.

Chief, I am sure that you read the article that was in the Washington Post on, I guess, it was Sunday. I was traveling, so I read all of my newspapers last night. But this was the one that is entitled, "The Firefighting Planes Have Been Perhaps on the Job Too Long." You have said a couple times here this morning that you believe that the resources are adequate, that what we have, whether it is equipment, or Senator Heller's son and others that are out fighting, or the air assets, that they are adequate.

The article makes a couple of statements here that I just want to ask you about. Large tanker planes leased by the agency that have been flying on average about 50 years are rapidly becoming unsafe to deploy. Then a statement about the 2009 report, and the Forest Service's replacement plan for aerial firefighter resources. According to the report, the remaining leased air tankers should fly for only one more year. After 2012, they will be too expensive to maintain or no longer air worthy, the Forest Service concluded.

So, the first question is whether or not you agree with that statement. Second question is, next year is next year, and we are working on the budget now, and we all know how long it takes to get anything around here. Are we going to be in a situation where next year we will not have air assets that you would consider adequate and/or safe? If that is the case, I would hope that we would not put the lives and the safety of those who are fighting our fires at risk. What is our plan? I know you said you are going to be getting this plan to us by the end of this summer, but are we not cutting this kind of close in terms of our preparedness?

Mr. TIDWELL. Senator, we have been continuing to work with our contractors to actually look at newer aircraft. They have been pursuing that to be able to bring on some newer aircraft. At the same time, we do hold them to very strict safety standards on the maintenance of these planes to ensure that they are not being flown unless they are safe, and that if—when I say we have adequate resources, if for some reason some planes needed to be grounded for maintenance or whatever, we have the ability to either bring on additional type one helicopters to replace those assets, or we can also make a request to our mass units from the National Guard to be able to offset that for a period of time.

We know that we need to lay out the strategy that will ensure that we have large air tankers as part of our resources into the future. That is what our strategy is going to be. It will have an interim approach so that we continue to work with, you know, our existing contractors or other contractors to be able to bring on aircraft that will continue to provide a period of time so that we do not have to, you know, wait 5 or 6 or 10 years to actually what we want in place for the foreseeable future.

So, it will be a combination of an interim strategy with a long-term strategy, and I remain confident that today that we have the adequate resources. But it is time for us to move forward, and that is why we will bringing that report recommendation to Congress, you know, later this summer so that we can begin the discussion about what is the best way to move forward with our recommendation.

Senator MURKOWSKI. When we had the discussion several months ago at Interior Approps, you assured me at that time that there was going to be a variety of aircraft types and sizes within the firefighting force. I take that to mean that it will be different brands. It will be including the size of heavy retardant aircraft, that this will be part of that mix. Is that a correct assumption?

Mr. TIDWELL. Senator, we need to look at every option that we have available. That is to look at a full range of the aircraft that are currently available and also some that are being currently developed. So, our strategy is going to look at using every option that is available for us to be able to continue to always have the resource that the large air tankers provide.

Senator MURKOWSKI. Good. It is good to hear that because since that hearing, there has been some feedback from some within the aircraft manufacturing companies and the companies that contract with the Forest Service. They have suggested that perhaps the heavy retardant aircraft would not be employed. But what I am hearing you say is that you are going to be looking to all options, including the heavy aircraft, the heavy retardant aircraft, and that will be included as part of the consideration, part of the mix.

Mr. TIDWELL. Yes.

Senator MURKOWSKI. OK. Let me ask then one final question. For a good part of the last decade, the Forest Service has refused to allow either the DC–10 or the Evergreen 747 to fly on the fires on national forest lands, but I see that this week, the Forest Service used the DC–10 in the Wallow fire. Has something changed? Are we going to be seeing more of these? Will we see them up in Alaska? What is the situation with the DC–10?

Mr. TIDWELL. We have had both the DC–10 and, in the past, the 747 under a call when needed contract. We have used them in the past. We did use the DC–10 on the Wallow fire. One of the things that we have asked the team to do as far as their after action review is to look at the effectiveness of very large aircraft, large air tanker, to help us learn, you know, especially in these type of fuel types, you know, the effectiveness of the drops that it made.

So, it is part of the mix of tools.

Senator MURKOWSKI. OK.

Mr. TIDWELL [continuing]. We are going to continue to have it available. When our incident commanders need that tool, they are going to order it.

Senator MURKOWSKI. As you look to rolling out this report here at the end of this season, will discussion about how the DC–10 performed be included as part of that review?

Mr. TIDWELL. We will be looking at what we call these very large air tankers, the DC–10 and the 747 to look at their effectiveness and, not only in the drops that they made, but also what type of terrain that they can be effective in.

Senator MURKOWSKI. Thank you, Mr. Chairman.

The CHAIRMAN. Senator Franken.

Senator FRANKEN. Thank you.

First of all, let me just say that I bring a great deal of humility to this subject. I am new to this committee this Congress, and, you know, on forest management, I certainly would yield to my friend who has a degree in forest management. I certainly do not.

But let me ask you about the scientists that you cited referring to the effect of climate change in the Forest Service. They have degrees, right?

Mr. TIDWELL. Yes.

Senator FRANKEN. Yes. Those degrees are like in what? The ones that you rely on for this information about the effect of climate change on forest fires? What would their degrees be in?

Mr. TIDWELL. They are in a variety of disciplines, primarily a focus on vegetation and understanding the effects of climate change on vegetation. We have the largest research and development operation—organization in the world when it comes to understanding natural resources. Where our focus is on understanding the effects of climate change, we rely on other entities to study the weather. So, our scientists are mostly focused on understanding these effects. That is what we have actually been doing research for now close to 30 years about the effects.

What our scientists have seen, how the vegetation have changed, you know, across the country and that we see where tree lines are, you know, moving higher up on to the slopes from what they were 20, 30, 40 years ago. The change in the vegetation, the change in the frequency of the disturbances, that is what we are focused on. That is what we are focused on, understanding those changes so that we can adapt our management to deal with these changes.

Senator FRANKEN. OK. So, in adapting the management, it is probably to say that Senator Risch might be right that we have made some mistakes in the past in terms of how we approach sustainable forests. Is that fair to say?

31

Mr. TIDWELL. I agree with Senator Risch that we need to be, you know, doing more work than we have done in the past. His point that he made about in the past there has been times that we have not been able to implement our projects because of lawsuits, that is true.

But what has changed today is that there is more and more agreement across the country, especially in our collaborative efforts where people have come together and understand the type of work that needs to be done. So, we are in a much better position today than we have been, I think, for a couple of decades to actually be able to move forward and to be able to implement the work on the ground that will make a difference.

Senator FRANKEN. In northeast Minnesota, we have a big forestry industry. I have seen exactly what you are saying at work. I have seen private and, you know, we have a paper company there, Blandin, which I have gone to, and they do sustainable forestry with the forests that they own. Part of that is actually harvesting certain fuel that does become fuel, and it becomes—in addition to becoming paper, it becomes fuel for, again, the kind of, you know, used as biomass.

Just following up on the question I asked before, do you think that across Federal, State, and private forests, we are adequately gathering and making use of this debris from the forest floor and other—not just debris on the forest floor, but of thinning of trees that—to use for this purpose?

Mr. TIDWELL. Senator, we are starting to be able to make use of this material, to put it to some beneficial use. But this is an area where we need considerable, I think, investment and additional facilities so that we can make more use of this material.

In the future, there is going to be a need to, you know, treat more acres. There is going to be a need to remove more of this material. So, the more than we can, you know, work with communities, work with private industry to be able to find ways that they can make the investment in these facilities, it will not only reduce the cost of removing the material from the national forests, but it will also put it to beneficial use and be able to create renewable energy.

Senator FRANKEN. Thank you. Thank you very much.

Mr. Chairman.

The CHAIRMAN. Senator Udall just arrived and has not had a chance to ask any questions. Senator Risch, is it OK if we go ahead and have Senator Udall ask his questions and then call on you? Is that acceptable?

Senator RISCH. I would be happy to yield.

The CHAIRMAN. Senator Udall, go right ahead.

Senator UDALL. Is the Senator from Idaho certain of that? We have a working relationship, and I do not want to do anything to change that.

Thank you——

Senator RISCH. You missed our discussion with Senator Franken about climate change, and it would have dovetailed nicely with our legislation on bark beetle infestations that we have in our two states.

Senator UDALL. I look forward to a complete report on the interchange between you and Senator Franken.

Senator RISCH. I do not think the problem—I do not think he—there was a disagreement in the problem. It was the cause of the problem that caused us to have a——

Senator UDALL. Senator Franken and I will continue to endeavor to convince you of our point of view, Senator Risch.

Senator RISCH. Please do. Please.

Senator UDALL. Chief, Secretary, thank you for being here. I was in a markup with an Armed Services subcommittee. This is the week in which we mark up the entire Armed Services authorization bill, so there is a lot going on. Thank you for your patience.

I know you visited with Senator Murkowski and Senator Wyden about aviation services. I think you know that I have been discussing this and drawing attention to it for a number of years, almost for a decade. I hope there is a solution in front of us.

But let me turn to a specific Colorado event that relates to aviation and aviation services. The Fourmile Canyon fire last year in Colorado was the most devastating in our history. A vast majority of that fire was not on Federal land, but Federal resources were brought in to fight it. There were, however, reports that it took more than 24 hours for the first aircraft to respond to the fire, and it came from across the State, while local resources were passed over.

I have asked you in the State to look into the issue and a variety of other concerns about the fire. We are doing a postmortem report, which I think will be very valuable as the ones in the past have been. But I think the question again rises, whether the Federal Government is using its aging resources in the most efficient way. Would you be willing to comment on this, and then Ms. Thorsen as well in turn, I would ask you to comment.

Mr. TIDWELL. Senator, with that fire, you know, it is my understanding, which is the case usually when we lose a fire during an initial attack, we had strong winds. I know it is difficult, especially for our communities in the public to understand that in high winds, the air tankers do not fly. They are not effective, and it is not safe. So, it is has been my experience that, and I think in this case the fire was a State fire working with the county there. They ordered the resources that they need, and it has my experience that our instant commanders, whether it is from the State or from Forest Service or any other agency, if they need a large air tanker, they are going to put an order in if they feel it is going to be effective. So, if the air tankers did not get there until the next day, you know, unless I have other information, I am going to assume that it was because of the weather they would not have been effective, or because of the terrain.

But we welcome the review. It is one of the things that we want to do, an after action review on all of our large fires so that we can continue to learn what we need to do. If there is a question about the resources that were not available, that is something we definitely need to look into.

But it has been my experience that our instant commanders order the resources that they need when they can be effective. But when we get the winds that we have normally around fires like you had experience there is that we are not able to fly. They are not effective. They are not safe. Large helicopters can fly in a little higher winds, but they, too—you know, over like 35, 40 miles an hour at the very most. We cannot fly aircraft.

Senator UDALL. I would just note that the issue—maybe I was not as clear as I might have been—was also in regards to helicopters and helicopter availability.

Ms. Thorsen, if you could respond briefly, if I could ask you so I could get a second question in during my 5 minutes, I would appreciate it.

Ms. THORSEN. Sure. I will keep it very short, Senator. I would agree with the chief, look forward to the review. I do not have any specifics on what happened on that fire, but we will certainly take what will come out of the review and ensure that we have got the processes in places. The ordering is very consistent and our folks do it all the time, so, as the chief said, I am sure it was the idiosyncrasies of the fire that kept them from doing that.

Senator UDALL. Thank you.

Ms. THORSEN. We will follow up.

Senator UDALL. I very much look forward to that.

Let me turn to mitigation. Of course, this has been a part of the conversation today. I know Senator Risch, Senator Bingaman, Senator Murkowski, myself, and everybody else who is here this morning have had the same look on our face that Senator Kyl had, which is a combination of horror and regret and commitment to doing more.

What are you doing about mitigation? What more can we do? I just met with a little company in Silver Plum, New Earth Pellets. They have developed a technique where they do not bring the trees to them, they take the drying machine to the tree and they turn the biomass into wood pellets. It is the most efficient way, I think, to turn that material into something useful. But if you would, in my remaining time, talk about mitigation and your plans.

Mr. TIDWELL. Senator, what you just mentioned is one of the examples that we need to work with private industry to, you know, find ways to increase our integrated wood products industry to make use of all of this material, whether it is the saw logs or the smaller diameter, you know, material.

The other key part of that is to be able to treat large enough acres where it really makes a difference. Then that has been our focus by using the Collaborative Landscape Forest Restoration Act projects that allow us to look at much larger landscapes, 50,000 acres. The work we are doing in Arizona with one of the projects there, we are pursuing to do one environmental impact statement to address 750,000 acres. This is what we need to do to be able to move forward, to be able to treat much larger areas.

It will also allow investment to occur. We want to continue to use our long-term stewardship contracts so that someone can realize that there is going to be a certain amount of work that is going to be done every year for like the next 10 years so that they can go ahead and make the investment in the equipment, like you just mentioned. That is a key tool that we need to continue to, you know, pursue.

We are working with CEQ to be able to pursue some pilot approaches to taking on this large-scale environmental analysis so that we have their support and their assistance.

These are some of the things that we are currently working on that I think will make a difference.

Senator UDALL. Thank you for that.

Mr. Chairman, I think two ideas that I have certainly heard would be to make the stewardship contract timeframe longer, something on the order of perhaps 15 or 20 years even. Now we have got to keep faith with the environmental laws.

Second, there is a very interesting idea circulating, and this is tied to the way OMB and CBO work, is that you would actually value the trees at zero dollars, and you would have more potential of getting the private sector involved. To me, it is counterintuitive, but I am really intrigued with that idea, and I would like to work with the committee.

Thank you, Mr. Chairman.

The CHAIRMAN. Thank you very much.

Senator Risch.

Senator RISCH. First of all, I agree with you, Senator Udall. Those are things that we really ought to have a look at.

The idea of a zero value tree I do not think is totally off the wall. Tom, correct me if I am wrong, but the Forest Service has done that. When we were in the road building business, frequently the cost of the roads exceeded the value of the timber or at least were a push. Am I right on that?

Mr. TIDWELL. Yes. Senator, we have currently readjusted our prices so that the average price of the material being removed is about where it was back in the early 1970s. So, it is something we are constantly focused on.

Our focus is to get the work accomplished. We do need to, when there is a value of the materials being removed, we need to ensure that the public is receiving the compensation for that. But that is another one of the key benefits of the stewardship contracting approach. Not only does it ensure that we take a collaborative approach to bring people together so that there is agreement on the type of work that needs to be done, but if there are any revenues that are produced from the trees, the biomasses removed, that can actually be put back into that project to be able to do more work, to be able to do more thinning, more watershed improvement, more fisheries work, whatever the project is designed to do.

Senator RISCH. I appreciate that. Tom, were you—you know, I appreciate your review of the fire in Arizona right now. Were you on the Biscuit fire over in Oregon, or did you happen to see the Biscuit fire over in Oregon? When was that, four years ago, five?

Mr. TIDWELL. No, it was longer than that, and I was not on that fire.

Senator RISCH. That was another one that was a real catastrophe. It got a lot of old growth timber. It got spotted owls. It got everything. I had really hoped that—and there was a lot of talk about it at the time that, oh, gosh, we learned a lot of lessons, and we are going to do this different, we are going to do that different. It does not seem—and that thing was such a catastrophe that I really thought that it would promote some changes, particularly in

35

fuel loading and doing the kind of management that you do to put strips in or what have you in order to stop the future fires.

But it does not seem like it resulted in anything. It came off of the front page, went to the second page, and then dropped out of the paper. We never heard about it again.

Any thoughts on that?

Mr. TIDWELL. Senator, I do think, you know, these large fires have helped to inform and encourage, you know, our communities, you know, people throughout this country to learn about the importance of forestry and the importance of restoring the resiliency of these systems.

I think the support that we have through our collaborative efforts today, I think they are a product of some of these that have happened in the past. I think, you know, the leadership that you provided there in Idaho to bring that group of folks together to be able to deal with the Idaho roadless rule. I think that has all helped.

So, I am going to stay optimistic that these things that have occurred in the past, we have learned from those. It has allowed us to be able to today to be able to have more agreement and be able to implement more work on the ground today than we have in the past. I think that three million acres that we treated last year, I think that is the byproduct from some of these events, some of these things that we have learned over time.

Senator RISCH. Thank you. That is an interesting perspective, and I guess I have to agree with you to a degree. That Biscuit fire destroyed, I think it was like 500,000 acres or something like that. It actually did not get controlled until the end of the December because of the snow, you know, obviously. It was kind of like the big burn really.

I tend to agree with you. I think that over time people are becoming more sensitive, as you know, in the roadless rule that you and I worked on together, and are still defending hopefully through just one more step.

I did see people more willing to talk about the urban interface area whereas before it was, you know, not one tree. In some of these areas that we would have had real trouble with, they agreed to removal of material in the urban interface area, which in Idaho is absolutely critical as you know because of a lot of small towns we have out there.

So, I appreciate your thoughts on that. That is an interesting point of view.

Thank you, Mr. Chairman.

The CHAIRMAN. Thank you.

Senator Murkowski, did you have additional questions?

Senator MURKOWSKI. No, thank you, Mr. Chairman.

The CHAIRMAN. Senator Udall, did you have additional questions?

Senator UDALL. Mr. Chairman, if I could, and you cut me off if necessary.

We have been talking about saw mills in Colorado. I do not know the situation in Idaho or New Mexico, but our saw mills, the few that we have are in real trouble. The significant reason behind that is that legacy timber sales are no longer financially viable and become a liability. I know Under secretary Sherman has been working on this. But what can we do to really resolve this issue? There has been a lot of talk, a lot of concern expressed. But, boy, the clock is running.

Mr. TIDWELL. Senator, with the mill you are referring to, I think it is the case in many parts of the country is that to be able to maintain this integrated wood products industry, there needs to be, you know, some certainty that the wood is going to be available. We definitely have the need on the landscape.

I want to go back to your earlier comment about, you know, stewardship contracting. Those long-term contracts have proven to be successful. The approach and the process that we use seems to be, one, it helps people to come together and reach agreement on the type of work. So, we are seeing fewer appeals, fewer lawsuits with those type of projects.

It is essential that, I think, we have that authority reauthorized. It is due to expire here in another 2 years, and it is just essential that as we move forward, that we continue to have that authority. I think that is going to continue to be one of the tools that we need to use and to be able to have that.

Senator UDALL. I want to follow up further with you on that, if I can. But not now, but, I think this is really an opportunity we could miss. I think it will be very hard to rebuild the saw mill sector.

Power lines. A big deal in Colorado. I do not know, again, about other western States, but we have one of the most populous western States, and we have a lot of electricity corridors running through our mountains.

Utilities have a point of view. You have a point of view. The projections are, and this is hard to believe, but more and more it has been confirmed, 100,000 trees a day coming down. That is mind boggling.

But we have got to get these negotiations concluded so that we can do the work to ensure these power line corridors are not going to either be subject to a fire because a tree falls on the line or because you have a problem with a line that then triggers the fire, and then those power lines are brought out of service. I know that is a big concern in Arizona.

So, I would just urge you to do everything possible to work out an agreement on the ground. A lot of this is tied to liability concerns, and I know the lawyers are important. I know Senator Risch is a lawyer.

Senator RISCH. Hear, hear.

Senator UDALL. I know Senator is a lawyer. I know Senator Bingaman is a lawyer. I do not want to be a lawyer.

But let us see if we can also bring some common sense to bear here and get a deal so we can move forward—and a lot of these power lines in Colorado are in the mountains. You cannot go in in the winter time and do that work. That is a plea to you, and any comment you would like to share with us, I would like to hear it.

Mr. TIDWELL. Senator, thank you for the letter you sent us. We are working on options, and we will have a response to you. I do think we have a couple of different options to be able to move forward to address that concern, and also at the same time, you know, satisfy the liability issue, too.

Senator UDALL. I have given the same speech to the utilities, by the way, so I am not just picking on you.

Mr. TIDWELL. They want to work with us, and I think it is just another opportunity that, by working together, not only can we ensure that, you know, their lines are protected that we all rely on, but at the same time, to be able to also get some additional restoration work done in areas that are adjacent to these lines.

Senator UDALL. Thank you for that.

Thanks, Mr. Chairman.

The CHAIRMAN. Senator Risch, did you have additional questions?

Senator RISCH. No, thank you. Thank you, Mr. Chairman.

The CHAIRMAN. We thank you both very much. You have been very generous with your time. It has been useful testimony. Thank you, and we wish you good luck the remainder of this fire season. Thank you.

Mr. TIDWELL. Thank you.

[Whereupon, at 11:40 a.m., the hearing was adjourned.]

APPENDIX

RESPONSES TO ADDITIONAL QUESTIONS

RESPONSE OF TOM TIDWELL TO QUESTION FROM SENATOR BINGAMAN

Question 1. A reference was made at the hearing to a pledge that every Forest Supervisor signed, reportedly to fully implement to 20 million acres the Healthy Forest Restoration Act. Can you describe for the Committee the pledge, its contents and the circumstances under which it was signed?

Answer. At a regular meeting with Forest Supervisors in early 2004, then-Chief Dale Bosworth was reviewing expectations for the coming year's hazardous fuels reduction efforts. As an impromptu show of support for the Chief and commitment to the agency's priorities, the meeting participants (the Supervisors from every National Forest) volunteered to a handwritten pledge to do all they can, within their authority, to meet the National Fuels target.

The 'pledge' made no reference to the Healthy Forests Restoration Act. As for acreages, no explicit acreage was mentioned, although one might infer from the President's FY2004 budget that the National Fuels target mentioned equates to 600,000 acres of hazardous fuels reduction treatments outside the wildland-urban interface, and 1,000,000 acres of hazardous fuels reduction treatments within the wildland-urban interface.

RESPONSES OF TOM TIDWELL TO QUESTIONS FROM SENATOR WYDEN

HAZARDOUS FUELS TREATED ACRES

Question 1. The Forest Service stated in the FY2012 budget justification that "naturally ignited fires that benefit the ecosystem will continue to be an important part of the total Hazardous Fuels program." Last year the Forest Service counted 150,000 acres of naturally ignited fires as hazardous fuels treated acres. This means that 57 percent of the acres that the USFS considered as treated for hazardous fuels were naturally ignited fires and were not typically thinned beforehand. Thinning forests and reintroducing fire is an important part of creating resilient forests. In 2010, the Pacific Northwest Research Station published a study of the 2006 Tripod Complex fires, demonstrating that an effective strategy to reduce future fire severity is to apply fuel treatments consisting of thinning forests followed by prescribed fire. The study demonstrated that in low elevation dry conifer forests, like the forests found in Oregon, 57 percent of trees that were previously thinned and burned with prescribed fire survived after a large wildfire. Whereas only 19 percent of trees that were in thin-only units survived the wildfire. I believe that it is important for the agency to mechanically reduce hazardous fuels, conduct prescribed fire treatments, and utilize forest byproducts to create jobs and support local mills. Chief Tidwell, please provide me details on how the agency will still make it a priority to apply fuel treatments to our forests that mechanically reduce fuels followed by prescribed fire treatments as opposed to simply relying on naturally ignited fires for the majority of acres considered treated.

Answer. About 160,000 acres of hazardous fuels were treated by wildfire in FY-2010. This represents less than 6 percent of the total National Forest System Lands treated for hazardous fuels that year. In contrast, about 1,170,000 acres of hazardous fuels were treated with mechanical means. About 75 percent of those acres included removal and utilization of the treatment by-products. Many of those acres will also be treated by prescribed fire in FY-2011.

Application of fuel treatments by mechanical means followed by prescribed fire treatments is an effective procedure and it is one of the most common methods that the Forest Service uses to reduce hazardous fuels. However, it is only one of the tools in our tool box. Other tools include prescribed fire as a single treatment and various mechanical manipulations as single treatments.

Using naturally ignited wildfires to accomplish fuel treatment objectives is an opportunistic scenario. We cannot chose the time or place of a naturally ignited wildfire. But occasionally lighting strikes in the right place, at the right time, and under the right conditions and we are able to accomplish resource objectives. Wildfire management decisions are made by on-the-ground fire managers in real-time, following carefully pre-designated guidelines and land and resource management plans. It is important that we provide fire managers the best resources and a wide range of options so that they may safely and effectively manage the wildfire.

APPRAISAL POINTS FOR TIMBER SALE SET ASIDES

Question 2. When the Forest Service sets the starting price for a timber sale minimum bid it "appraises" the sale price based on the transportation cost to haul logs to the nearest mill. When a timber sale is set aside for small business, the Forest Service still applies this same rule. Yet whenever a sale is set aside for small business, at least 70 percent of the logs by volume must be delivered to a small business mill, wherever one is. These logs are not allowed to be delivered to a large business mill, even if a large business mill is closer to the sale location. The 70 percent rule is a requirement of the Small Business Administration regulations in 13 CFR 121.507(a)(3). The 70 percent requirement, combined with the Forest Service "nearest mill" appraisal policy, puts small business timber purchasers in a bind. The small business timber purchasers do not get a break on the sale appraisal for having these extra transportation costs. I would like to know if the Forest Service can give small business purchasers relief from high transportation costs on sales set aside for small business, by adopting the nearest small business mill as the "appraisal point." Can the Forest Service do this within its administrative authority? Or does this need legislation to fix the problem?

Answer. As noted the 30/70 rule is a SBA regulation that applies to small businesses. It is designed to help small business sawmills and is specifically for saw logs. It also applies to small business non-manufacturers (generally independent loggers) who purchase timber sales and then dispose of the logs. Appraisal points are selected to provide an estimate of fair market value for all of industry. Any changes in timber sales policies that affect small businesses are to be published in the Federal Register for public comments in accordance with Congressional direction. Presently, the Forest Service is analyzing the different small business areas around the country to determine the extent of the situation. The Forest Service intends to publish a proposed policy in the Federal Register late this year that will consider changes to the appraisal point.

RESPONSES OF TOM TIDWELL TO QUESTIONS FROM SENATOR UDALL

Question 1. Colorado's last large sawmill—Intermountain Resources in Montrose, Colorado—is in severe financial trouble and could close in the immediate future. Losing this mill would be a heavy blow to our forest products industry and our efforts to combat the bark beetle epidemic and implement fuels treatments across the state. Without Intermountain mill in Montrose as a processing location, the distance to the next closest mill with capacity to process any meaningful volumes of beetle-kill timber is nearly 800 miles away in Montana.

While there are a number of reasons that the mills are failing, one significant reason is that they hold legacy U.S. Forest Service (USFS) timber sales that are no longer financially viable and have become a financial liability. The good news is that the USFS can play a vital role in helping this mill survive. In October 2010, Undersecretary Sherman visited Montrose and committed the USFS to exploring every option to help save the critical timber industry. Unfortunately, since that time very little has been done:

I understand that the USFS offered contract changes under the Market Related Contract Term Adjustment (MRCTA), but that only two of 51 contracts qualified because most of the legacy timber sales are classified "urgent removal," and thus do not qualify under MRCTA (please note that almost all of the offering portfolio in Colorado in recent years has been classified as "urgent removal" because sales were targeted to beetle-kill and Wildland Urban Interface (WUI) areas).

a. Is that accurate? Beyond these contract changes, what else is the Forest Service doing to help resolve this issue?

Answer. On August 2, 2011, Chief Tidwell signed a Decision Memo regarding high priced sales in Region 2 that were sold prior to July 2008 that will allow the Forest Service and a timber sale purchaser in Region 2 to agree to mutually cancel a timber sale. Prior to this date the Forest Service had allowed all the relief that was qualified under the timber sale contract.

41

Question 2. Regarding the bark beetle epidemic, I understand that the Forest Service is developing a Western Bark Beetle Strategy. Can you tell me about this strategy? When will it be completed?

Answer. The Western Bark Beetle Strategy identifies how the Forest Service is responding to and will respond to the western bark beetle epidemic over the next five years. The extent of the epidemic requires prioritization of treatments, first providing for human safety in areas threatened by standing dead hazard trees, and second, addressing dead and down trees that create hazardous fuels conditions adjacent to high value areas. After the priority of safety, forested areas with severe mortality will be reforested with the appropriate species (Recovery). Forests will also be thinned to reduce the number of trees per acre and create more diverse stand structures to minimize extensive epidemic bark beetle areas (Resiliency). This is a modest strategy that reflects current budget realities, but focuses our resources in the most important places where we can make a big difference to the safety of the American public. This strategy covers Fiscal Year (FY) 2011 through 2016. The Strategy is completed and going through clearance.

RESPONSES OF TOM TIDWELL TO QUESTIONS FROM SENATOR MURKOWSKI

Question 1. Please have your researchers develop an estimate of what the total cost of the fires in 2002 and 2010 were.

Answer. The impacts of wildland fires on local, regional and national economic well being are very complex and vary greatly depending on the characteristics of the event (fire extent, intensity, duration, proximity to human development, community resource dependency, ecological conditions and many others).

The Western Forestry Leadership Council recently released a report summarizing the range of economic costs identified within the literature for a small number of the larger wildfire events of the past decade (see "The True Cost of Wildland Fire", 2009). The fires considered within this summary report show total economic cost ranging from 2 to 30 times the total suppression costs. However, it should be recognized that each of the studies reviewed in this document required considerable resources to summarize the economic impacts of a single event and the study highlights the significant range of outcomes. Most of the fires evaluated in this report had significant suppression resources assigned and yet wildfire extent and economic losses were considerable.

The application of the "total cost" evaluation process requires the acquisition of considerable event specific information from numerous data sources and substantial analyses which is impossible to complete for every fire in a given year due to the sheer volume of fires the agency manages. We do believe that an understanding of the total economic costs of these events is very relevant and improved information could yield improved policy. The agency will continue to support research to determine methods to evaluate total wildfire costs in a rapid and consistent method for large fires.

A goal of wildfire management is to reduce the long term losses associated with wildland fires and the agency's adoption of risk management principles emphasizes the balancing of fiscal cost and risk to firefighters and public interests.

Question 2. During an active Alaska fire season, approximately how much is expended to transport and house the fire crews from the lower 48 to assist Alaska fire crews in suppressing fires?

Answer. (Note to Reviewers: This was developed by DOI staff at NIFC in response to the same question, it should not be edited to ensure consistency).

We have a transport jet on Federal contract for the express purpose of mobilizing crews when and where they are most needed across the nation. The total cost spent on moving crews to or from Alaska will vary per year depending on fire activity and need. However, for 2011, the federally contracted Boeing 737 can mobilize five 20-person crews, equaling 100 persons, from Boise to Alaska for approximately $26,000.00, or $260.00 per firefighter; or $520.00 round trip.

The cost to transport, feed, and house the crews while in Alaska is the same per-person cost as Alaska Type 2 crews.

Question 3. Would it cost more each year to transport the crews from the lower 48 back and forth to Alaska, or to invest in the training to increase the qualifications of the Native Crews?

Answer. The U.S. Forest Service does not sponsor any Emergency Fire Fighting crews in Alaska and is consequently not well suited to address this question. However, the U.S. Department of Interior Bureau of Land Management, which includes the Alaska Fire Service, is preparing a response to it.

Question 4. For the last decade Australia, France, Greece, Spain, Italy, Canada, the States of Alaska, California, Washington, and Minnesota have all used the Canadian Bombardier CL-415 amphibious water-scooping aircraft to drop water and foam on fires. The aircraft has proven to be quite successful. Yet, the Forest Service has steadfastly refused to even test these airplanes on federal fires.

At the same time the agency has been tangled up in court over the use of slurry and stands to lose the ability to use the retardant if the Judge in Montana rules against its use.

> a. Can you explain to me why the Forest Service refuses to use the water scooping fire fighting aircraft?

Answer. The FS uses Scooper aircraft through its cooperator agencies when appropriate.

> b. Can you tell me what your agency's plans are if Judge Malloy in Montana outlaws the use of slurry for wildland fire fighting?

Answer. We will comply with the court decision. If retardant could no longer be used, we would rely more on water dropping aircraft.

> c. Is Congress going to have to put legislative language in an appropriations bill to require your agency to provide alternatives to the Lockheed C-130 J?

Answer. No. The Forest Service is evaluating all available options.

> d. If we agree that you recently indicated to me there will be a variety of types and sizes of heavy retardant aircraft, will you instruct the employees in your fire and aviation group to reflect that commitment in their discussions with your heavy retardant vendors and the air craft manufacturing companies?

Answer. Yes.

> e. If we cannot agree on the premise of Question 4(d), will you please inform the Secretary of Agriculture that he and I need to have a discussion on the future expenditures on aerial firefighting that your agency undertakes?

Answer. The Forest Service agrees with the premise of Question 4(d).

Question 5. Contractors have indicated that if offered the ability to enter into long term contracts—such as ten years—they could facilitate financing of re-winged or even new aircraft for the aerial firefighting fleet.

> f. Does the U.S. Forest Service (USFS) have the authority to enter into long-term contracts with providers of aerial firefighting services? If so, please provide the statutory citations for this authority.

Answer. We have the authority for 5 years, but not for 10 years[1].

> g. If the Forest Service does not have the authority to enter into long-term contracts, would you welcome enactment of a statute providing you with that authority?

Answer. Yes. Longer term contracts may provide an incentive for contractors to purchase or upgrade their aircraft.

Question 6. Section 8118 of the House FY 2011 Continuing Appropriations Act (H.R. 1) called for a report that studies the purchase by the federal government of up to 24 new C-130J aircraft to be operated by the Air National Guard— effectively replacing the fleet of contractor-owned and contractor-operated aircraft now used as first responders to combat forest fires.

> h. How much do you anticipate it will cost the USFS to acquire the 24 new C-130J aircraft called for in the study?

Answer. The 2010 Act had similar language and Paul Stockton, Assistant Secretary of Defense on May 15, 2011, said that this mission was not viable. Therefore, the Forest Service has not prepared an estimate of the cost to acquire 24 new C-130J aircraft to be operated by the Air National Guard.

> i. I understand that contractors position their airtankers at various locations throughout country during the fire season, and that depending on the fire conditions, the fleet is repositioned to provide effective coverage across the country. If the Air National Guard owns and operates our country's aerial firefighting aircraft, where will these aircraft be positioned during the fire season?

Answer. Not applicable per response above.

---

[1] Section 205 of Public Law 78–425 (16 U.S.C. 579a)

j. If the aircraft are located at National Guard airbases, how would you handle coverage of areas such as the state of Alaska that are far from these airbases?

Answer. Not applicable per response above.

k. Flying firefighting missions is a highly specialized task, which takes hours of training, and for which relatively few pilots are sufficiently trained. How will the USFS handle the training of Air National Guard pilots for such missions, and what retention strategies will be implemented to assure that these pilots continue to participate in firefighting missions after they have receive this specialized training?

Answer. Not applicable per response above.

l. What will be the cost to the taxpayer of training and retaining pilots for the mission of fighting forest fires?

Answer. Not applicable per response above.

m. What guarantee do we have that aircraft owned by the National Guard for the purposes of combating forest fires will not be diverted overseas for national security purposes?

Answer. Not applicable per response above.

n. Over the last ten years, how many drops of retardant on actual fires have been executed by the Air National Guard? Please do not include in this calculation any drops that were delivered by the Air National Guard during training exercises.

Answer. Between 2000 and 2009 the Air National Guard and Air Force Reserve flew 3635 sorties with a high of 851 in 2000 and a low of 0 in 2009. The actual number of sorties flown depends on the intensity of the fire season and availability of other contracted firefighting support, since this program is used when other contracted support is not available.

Year Sorties Flown

2000	851
2001	200
2002	637
2003	62
2004	260
2005	368
2006	613
2007	74
2008	570
2009	0
2010	4

o. How many personnel will be dedicated by the Air National Guard for the operation and maintenance of each of the aircraft envisioned to be purchased for use in fighting forest fires?

Answer. Not applicable per response above.

Question 7. Does the Forest Service support replacing the current contractor-owned, contractor-operated fleet of heavy air tankers with new C-130Js to be purchased by the taxpayer and operated by the Air National Guard?

Answer. Assistant Secretary of Defense Stockton stated this is not viable.

Question 8. Before developing a position regarding the long term replacement of the current heavy air tanker fleet, will the Forest Service study, and provide this

Subcommittee with an analysis of each of the following? (For each item listed below, please answer yes or no.)

a. The cost of alternative aircraft, including Casa 235s, C-130Hs, re-winged P-3s, and other alternatives.

Answer. Yes

b. The effectiveness of various aircraft capable of use as heavy tankers and respective tanking systems.

Answer. Yes

c. The relative costs of having the aircraft owned by the government as opposed to financed and owned by the private sector.

Answer. Yes

d. The relative costs and effectiveness of having the aircraft operated by private companies as opposed to by the Air National Guard.

Answer. Assistant Secretary of Defense Stockton stated this is not viable

e. The potential for aircraft owned and operated by the Air National Guard being diverted for use for National Security needs, and the consequences of such diversion.

Answer. Assistant Secretary of Defense Stockton stated this is not viable

f. The concept of pre-positioning heavy tankers in the vicinity of high risk/highly populated areas such as Southern California.

Answer. Yes.

g. The current systems in place for repositioning aircraft and ordering their use for combating specific fires, and whether such systems can be improved.

Answer. Yes.

RESPONSES OF TOM TIDWELL TO QUESTIONS FROM SENATOR BARRASSO

Question 1. At the public land subcommittee hearing held on May 25th, both Under Secretary Harris Sherman and Deputy Director Marcilynn Burke supported good neighbor authority. In Colorado alone, Mr. Sherman testified the authority has been used successfully on 37 projects covering 3,900 acres. These projects focused on fuel reduction within the wild land-urban interface.

a. Had my Good Neighbor Forestry Bill been signed into law last year, as it was introduced, would it have aided the forest service in dealing with the terrible forest fuels problems that have been occurring? BLM?

b. How many more acres might have been treated if Good Neighbor authority was available to the Forest Service? BLM?

Answer. The Good Neighbor Authority for use in Colorado was enacted in the 2000 Interior Appropriations Act and was extended most recently to September 30, 20013. The similar Good Neighbor authority for use in Utah was enacted in the Consolidated Appropriations Act for 2005 and was extended most recently to September 30, 2011. Both Good Neighbor Authorities authorize cooperative projects between USFS and the states of Utah and Colorado. Except as otherwise indicated, both Authorities include the following provisions with regard to projects being implemented under the umbrella of the Good Neighbor Authority:

Any decision required to be made under NEPA may not be delegated to the State.

- A cooperative agreement or contract to implement a project may authorize the State Forester to serves as the agent for the USFS.
- In Colorado, projects on National Forest System lands may be implemented when similar or complimentary treatments are being implemented on adjacent State or private lands.

a. The Good Neighbor Forestry Act (S. 1122) would have provided the US Forest Service with another tool to address hazardous fuels on National Forest System lands in states west of the 100th meridian.

b. The Forest Service has good relationships with State Foresters. There are several tools at the agency's disposal, such as State Fire Assistance grants and authority to spend some hazardous fuels money to treat non-Federal land. Additionally, since there is often a significant amount of time needed to plan, coordinate, and document projects before they can be implemented, I do not know how many additional acres might have been treated.

Question 2. There are now 3.6 million acres of mountain pine beetle infestation in Wyoming alone. Given the likelihood of high intensity fires associated with beetle kill, what policy or decision making changes does the Forest Service employ in high beetle kill areas when dealing with wildfire?

Answer. The Forest Service has placed a high priority on treating the hazardous fuels in beetle kill areas, especially when also in the Wildland Urban Interface. The Rocky Mountain Region, which includes Colorado and Wyoming, has created a special task force to coordinate funding and activities between FS resource emphasis areas and administrative units to most effectively address the hazards posed by beetle killed trees.

Question 3. The Forest Service has sought C-130 Fire Fighting Capabilities. In the "Report on the Joint Use of Federal Forest Fire Fighting Assets/C-130 Fire Fighting Capabilities" dated February 9, 2011, the report states:

> The Department of Defense believes that the mission proposed in the explanatory statement is not viable. DoD has critical concerns regarding the additional manpower and financial resources that would be required for the Air Force Reserve and Air National Guard to accomplish this mission in other than a secondary role.

Other options have proven effective at wild land fire suppression including the use of refurbished surplus military aircraft and the use of private sector capabilities.

> c. Given the DoD believes the use of C-130s is not viable, what is being done to retrofit and extend the life of existing P-3s? Answer—An extensive airworthiness oversight program is in place to monitor the status of the aircraft. The Forest Service has no plans to extend the life of the existing P-3s.
> d. What has the Forest Service done to find or encourage replacement aircraft and service crews from the private sector?

Answer. We are working with the commercial airtanker industry as part of our strategy to ensure availability of safe and cost efficient aerial firefighting aircraft.

Responses to our Request for Information (RFI) for the 2012 season have been received. We are in the process of developing a Request for Proposals (RFP). Draft technical specifications for the RFP have been developed and are currently under review. The proposed contract format would be an exclusive Firm Fixed Price Multiyear contract not to exceed five years. The RFP will target newer technology aircraft.

Question 4. In 2010, Richard Lasko, Forest Service Assistant Director for Fire and Aviation Management, Fuels and Fire Ecology wrote:

> A Revision of the 2003 Interagency Strategy removes the distinction between wild land fire use and wildfire. This will enhance a fire manager's ability to implement Federal Wild land Fire Management Policy by allowing consideration of the full range of positive and negative attributes of a fire"

I appreciate every fire can be both beneficial and detrimental. However, with dry conditions in the Southwest, and beetle kill timber in many states including Wyoming, there are environmental and resource risks associated with allowing fires to burn.

> e. In Forests like the Medicine-Bow National Forest with its high beetle kill, is it prudent to allow any wild land fire use when in all likelihood they will be high intensity fires?
> f. If yes, how does the Forest Service make the determination?

Answer. Decisions to use naturally ignited wildfires to accomplish fuel treatment objectives are based on local conditions. Prior to local fire seasons, fire management teams collaborating with other Federal, State, and local agency partners determine where naturally ignited wildfires may provide resource benefits and whether they would meet desired future conditions as stated in forest plans.

Wildfire management decisions are made by on-the-ground fire managers in real-time. Every effort is made to provide them the best resources and a wide range of options so that they may safely and effectively manage wildfires. If conditions are not right (e.g. too dry, too much wind, resources are committed elsewhere, too close to valued resources, etc.), field managers will not attempt to accomplish broader resource objectives. All fire managers understand that the standing priorities for managing wildfires are protection of human lives and property. U.S. Forest Service Interim Guidance For Wildfire Response (April 2011), issued to wildfire managers, stipulates the following:

1. All wildfires will have a protection objective. Incorporate the potential for threat to life and property in initial and subsequent courses of action on every fire.

2. A wildfire may be concurrently managed for more than one objective.

3. Unplanned natural ignitions may be managed to achieve Land and Resource Management Plan objectives when risk is within acceptable limits. Risk is elevated and uncertain on longer duration incidents.

4. Human caused fires and trespass fires will continue to be suppressed safely and cost effectively and will not be managed for resource benefits.

RESPONSES OF TOM TIDWELL TO QUESTIONS FROM SENATOR HELLER

Question 1. Chief Tidwell, thank you for your testimony. As a new member of this committee I want you to know that this issue is very important to me from my state's perspective in fighting forest fires. One of the three contractors providing the Forest Service with heavy air tanker service is located in Minden, NV.

I know Minden Air has been contracting with the Forest Service for many years and are using their experience, aviation background and own capital to develop a new platform based on the BAE-146 to help the Forest Service find a next generation platform for aerial firefighting needs. I hope that you will continue to work with them as they go through the process to certify this new aircraft and put a strong and viable option on the table for the Forest Service as it looks to the future of the heavy air tanker. Will you please keep me updated on your ongoing relationship with Minden Air and their role in future firefighting strategies?

Answer. Yes.

Question 2. As I mentioned earlier, the results of pre-treatment in the Lake Tahoe Basin provide an important return on the investment. What plans do the Forest Service have to insure that the Lake Tahoe Basin has the resources it needs to protect the people, structures and ecosystem through preventative treatments?

Answer. The Lake Tahoe Basin Multi-Jurisdictional Fuel Reduction and Wildfire Prevention Strategy of 2007 Strategy identifies how the Forest Service in collaboration with other land agencies will reduce the probability of a catastrophic fire in the Basin the next 10 years. It was developed to comply with the White Pine County Conservation, Recreation, and Development Act of 2006 (Public Law 109-432 [H.R.6111]). It comprehensively combines all existing plans that have been developed within the Basin, and provides a framework for participating agencies to identify priority areas and a strategy to work collaboratively on accomplishing those priorities. The plan recognizes that wildfire protection in the Basin requires three components:

- Buildings and homes should be built of fire-resistant materials and have effective defensible space;
- Accumulations of hazardous vegetative fuels must be reduced in the areas directly adjacent to communities; and
- Accumulations of vegetative hazardous fuels surrounding the Community Defensible Space should be reduced in the general forest. Treatments include thinning, pruning, prescribed burning, mastication and chipping.

Implementation of this plan is predicted to cost from $206,000,000 to $244,000,000 over 10 years. At the national level, the Forest Service uses a computer model to inform allocation of hazardous fuel funding to the regions. This model includes consideration of wildfire potential, resource values that are threatened by wildfire, program performance, and coordination with other programs. The Pacific Southwest Region, which includes the Lake Tahoe Basin, routinely gets the highest allocation of all the regions. The regions then distribute their allocation to the units (forests) using similar criteria.

Question 3. The personal impacts of wildfire are a huge burden to my constituents. I have heard story after story of folks who have watched a fire burn on public lands, been prevented from putting the fire out, only to see it eventually destroy their property.

As you know, if a private party starts a fire that spreads to public lands, they are held accountable. Whereas, if the federal government starts or fails to aggressively suppress a fire that destroys private property—there is vastly less accountability. In light of this, what are the trends in wildland use fires over the last 5 years? And, what percentage of catastrophic wildfires were designated as wildland use fires instead of aggressively suppressed?

Answer. The following table displays the acres of hazardous fuels treated by wildfire for each of the last five years:

Year	Acres of hazardous fuels treated by wildfire
2010	164,200
2009	309,900
2008	221,800
2007	290,228
2006	172,100

From the figures in the table above, there is no discernable trend. The resulting trend may be flat or constant. For comparison, the following table shows the total number of acres burned by wildfires and the total number of acres burned by wildfires on National Forest System (NFS) lands.

Year	Total Number of Acres burned by wildfire	Number of Acres burned by wildfire on NFS lands
2010	3,422,700	319,700
2009	5,921,786	715,700
2008	5,292,500	1,234,500
2007	9,328,000	2,835,600
2006	9,873,700	1,896,100

The Forest Service stopped designating wildfires as "wildland use fires" and stopped using the term "Wildland fire use" in 2009. In the previous years, in 2008 2.4 percent of all wildfires were declared wildland fire use, in 2007 that number was 2.3 percent, and in 2006 it was 2.5 percent.

The current wildfire policy provides field managers the widest possible flexibility to manage wildfires safely, effectively, and to use available resources efficiently. It is only after the wildfire is out that the impacts are compared to the desired conditions described in the applicable forest plan. If the wildfire effectively treated the hazardous fuels, helped meet the desired condition, and met the other criteria related to beneficial impacts from wildfire then the results are recorded as hazardous fuels treated by wildfire.

———

RESPONSES OF KIM THORSEN TO QUESTIONS FROM SENATOR MURKOWSKI

Question 1. Please have your researchers develop an estimate of what the total cost of the fires in 2002 and 2010 were.

Answer. The total cost of fires is a difficult question to answer, especially for large fires that significantly impact structural and natural resources. The impacts of wildland fires on local, regional and national economic well being are very complex and vary greatly depending on the characteristics of the event (fire extent, intensity, duration, proximity to human development, community resource dependency, ecological conditions and many others).

The Western Forestry Leadership Council recently released a report summarizing the range of economic costs identified within the literature for a small number of the larger wildfire events of the past decade (see "The True Cost of Wildland Fire", 2009). The fires considered within this summary report show total economic cost ranging from 2 to 30 times the total suppression costs. However, it should be recognized that each of the studies reviewed in this document required considerable resources to summarize the economic impacts of a single event and the study highlights the significant range of outcomes. Most of the fires evaluated in this report had significant suppression resources assigned and yet wildfire extent and economic losses were considerable.

The application of the "total cost" evaluation process requires the acquisition of considerable event specific information from numerous data sources and substantial analyses which is impossible to complete for every fire in a given year due to the sheer volume of fires the agency manages. We do believe that an understanding of the total economic costs of these events is very relevant and improved information could yield improved policy. The agency will continue to support research to determine methods to evaluate total wildfire costs in a rapid and consistent method for large fires.

A goal of wildfire management is to reduce the long term losses associated with wildland fires and the agency's adoption of risk management principles emphasizes the balancing of fiscal cost and risk to firefighters and public interests.

Question 2. During an active Alaska fire season, approximately how much is expended to transport and house the fire crews from the lower 48 to assist Alaska fire crews in suppressing fires?

Answer. The Department of the Interior spends approximately $180,000 to transport crews annually to support Alaska fires. The costs to feed and house these crews are consistent with the cost of Alaska crews and mostly reflect fire line meals and camp rate.

Fire crews are transported to Alaska during an active fire season to fill crew orders that cannot be filled within Alaska. These orders are typically for specialty crews like Type 1 or Type 2 IA crews that can be broken down into smaller groups for initial attack. The number is dependent on the availability of local crews and incident commander's specific needs.

The Alaska Fire Service transports, on an average, 16 crews per year to support fires in Alaska. The range is from 2 Type 1 crews in 2008 to 39 Type I and Type 2 IA crews in 2004. We have a transport jet on federal contract for the express purpose of mobilizing crews when and where they are most needed across the nation. For 2011, the federally contracted Boeing 737 can mobilize five 20-person crews, equaling 100 persons, from Boise to Alaska for approximately $26,000.00, or $260.00 per firefighter; or $520.00 round-trip. The total cost spent on moving crews to or from Alaska will vary per year depending on fire activity and need. Based on the annual average of 16 crews per year the cost would be approximately $180,000.

The cost to feed, and house the crews while in Alaska is minimal because of fire assignments and is consistent with costs of mobilizing and supporting Alaska Native Crews. They are provided with fire line meals and camp out.

Question 3. Would it cost more each year to transport the crews from the lower 48 back and forth to Alaska, or to invest in the training to increase the qualifications of the Native Crews?

Answer. It would cost considerably more to invest in training and outfitting Type 1 crews in Alaska than simply using the national mobilization system to fill Alaska's crew needs. Three type 1 crews are currently trained and maintained in the State of Alaska, including two managed by the Alaska Fire Service and one managed by the Alaska Department of Forestry. On average, 13 Type I crews per year are transported from the lower 48 to support fires in Alaska. A type 1 crew costs approximately $500,000 per year to train and outfit. The cost to train and outfit 13 additional Type 1 crews in Alaska would be approximately $6.5 million. The cost of mobilizing 13 existing Type 1 crews from the lower 48 would be approximately $156,000.

The Department is very supportive of cost effective crew development and utilization. The Alaska Fire Service (AFS) has an established program in place that is designed to train village crews as the primary firefighting force in Alaska. The AFS manages an Emergency Firefighter (EFF) program that consists of 73 Type 2 crews in 49 villages. This results in an average annual payroll of $8.3 million to local villages. Crews are managed under the Alaska Emergency Firefighter Type 2 Crew Management Guide, Revised March 2010 and available at http://fire.ak.blm.gov/logdisp/crews.php. The guide is produced by the EFF Crew Management Board which is a subgroup of the Alaska Wildland Fire Coordinating Group's Operations Committee.

In recent years, an average of 35 Type 2 crews per year were sent from Alaska to lower 48 assignments, as well as utilizing them on multiple in state assignments. Village crews within Alaska are a powerful and useful firefighting tool, and the AFS works very diligently to keep them trained and available for use throughout Alaska and the Continental US.

During periods of high fire activity, Incident Commanders can and do order agency "hotshot" crews to fill critical assignments or protect high value resources. Moving firefighting resources to areas of highest priority is a common business practice throughout the country, and one that we believe ultimately saves money for the agencies and taxpayers.

49

The Alaska Fire Service is cognizant of the cost of-moving resources to the state, and works hard to use the practice only when necessary. The Alaska Fire Service is currently working with the State of Alaska, and Native Corporations within the Alaska Wildfire Coordinating Group (AWFCG), to provide greater opportunities for additional firefighter training. This additional training will be used to create a local pool of Type 2 IA crews that can supplement the traditional roster of Type 2 village crews. This will help to reduce the need to mobilize T2 IA crews from the lower 48.

As noted, we have invested in expanding our training in Alaska in recent years to increase the qualifications of those crews.

Question 4a. Over the last two decades, the Bureau of Land Management seems to have made the decision to focus its aerial fire fighting resources on the small single engine aircraft commonly called the SEATS aircraft.

In making the decision to focus on the single-engine SEATS aircraft, the BLM opted not to use the heavy multi-engine aircraft the Forest Service has chosen; how did the Bureau of Land Management make its decision?

Answer. The Bureau of Land Management, as well as the other bureaus within the Department of the Interior (DOI) with fire management responsibilities (Bureau of Indian Affairs, Fish and Wildlife Service, and National Park Service) and the Forest Service use Large Airtankers (LATS), Single Engine Airtankers (SEATS), water scoopers and helicopters to deliver water, water with foam or other water enhancers and water with retardant to extinguish fires or retard their growth. Fire Managers, regardless of agency, use the most appropriate aviation resource for the mission requirements. The perception that one agency prefers to use LATS and another SEATS is an unintended artifact of agreed to interagency business protocols for contracting efficiencies and does not reflect actual fire management operations.

Factors that determine which aviation resources are utilized on a particular fire, regardless of agency responding, include: speed, range, capacity, suitability for the terrain, operating altitude and suitability for the mission. The diversity model allows DOI and Forest Service fire managers to apply the "right tool to the job" and all five federal agencies use all types of available aviation resources.

—Large Airtankers (FATS) have the advantage of speed and capacity to the target. Their range allows for rapid deployment over long distances enabling them to reinforce operations across geographic boundaries. They also deliver large amounts of water/retardant in one mission, often in locations where other options are unavailable.
—Single Engine Airtankers (SEATs) have the advantage of mobility and maneuverability. The infrastructure required to fuel and load SEATs is relatively minimal in terms of size and cost. This allows SEATs to operate close to the fire, shortening turn-around times and thereby increasing effectiveness. Due to their small size, SEATs are capable of great accuracy in rough terrain. SEATs also have the advantage of being "purpose-designed" to accurately dispense payload in the low altitude flight regime encountered during the wildland firefighting mission.
—Water scoopers have the advantage of speed and capacity, when there are appropriate water sources close to the fire site.
—Helicopters have the advantage of large and sustained capacity for personnel and cargo movement. Helicopter delivery of firefighters, either helitack or rappellers, and supplies has the advantage of speed and accuracy. Helicopters have the versatility for multiple missions including personnel and cargo movement, command and control and aerial ignition operations. And, helicopter delivery of water/retardant has the advantage of accuracy, speed, capacity, and increased water/retardant drop frequency if water resources are close to the fire site.

The aviation resources available to support the federal agencies for wildfire management are a mix of government owned/government operated and vendor owned/vendor operated aircraft There are relatively few government owned/government operated aircraft in the agencies' fleet and these are most often special use aircraft such as smokejumper aircraft and lead planes. To further increase effectiveness of contracting aerial firefighting resources, the Forest Service agreed to contract for large air tankers for use by all federal agencies, and the Department of the Interior's Aviation Management Directorate (AMD) has agreed to contract single engine air tankers for use by all agencies. The AMD also contracts for CL-215 larger water-scooping air tankers for use in Alaska (exclusive use contract) and the lower 48 (call-when-needed contract).

Question 4b. In that process, did the Bureau of Land Management hold a competition to learn which brand and model of aircraft best met the needs of the Bureau's fire fighters?

Answer. To achieve the right mix of air assets necessary to meet the diverse requirements of the wildland firefighting mission, the Department of the Interior focuses our contract specifications on the qualities and capabilities that best meet our fire response needs. We focus on required performance, not aircraft brands or models. The effectiveness of aviation resources on a fire is directly proportional to the speed and frequency at which the resource(s) can initially engage the fire, and the effective water/retardant carrying capacity of the aircraft. These factors are magnified by flexibility in prioritization, mobility, positioning and utilization of the versatility of many types of aircraft. Allowing any single element of the aviation resource mix to be dominated by one make and model of aircraft puts that entire element at danger of shutdown when and if an airworthiness issue is raised with that particular make and model of aircraft. Reliance on one make/model aircraft also limits the leverage the government has in managing contract costs with vendors.

The maintenance, parts supply and other efficiencies that private enterprise might gain from operating one make and model of aircraft are unlikely to be achieved in a fleet of the size and composition of the one that wildland agencies currently manage. Diversity of the fleet means a mix of types of aircraft with specific mission strengths that provide a toolbox for fire managers to use with specific fire situations.

Aviation resources are available nationwide to the federal agencies as a mix of different aircraft that may include large fixed-wing air tankers (LATs), smaller single engine fixed wing air tankers (SEATs), large and small helicopters, smaller fixed wing aircraft, and smokejumper aircraft. The relative mix of these aircraft on any given fire is determined by several factors including the type, location, and duration of incidents. The infrastructure necessary to support any of the aviation elements must also be included in any decision as to the numbers, location and utilization of that particular resource.

Aviation resources that require significant capital investment, software, analysis and training to be fully functional are by nature less flexible than those that require little or no upfront investment. Analysis of the optimum mix and number of aircraft includes these costs.

Question 4c. Does the Bureau of Land Management restrict their contracts to a single model manufactured by a single aircraft manufacturer or does the agency allow multiple companies to bid as long as the aircraft offered meets the contract specifications?

Answer. Contracts are not restricted to aircraft model or manufacturer, but rather to aircraft performance characteristics designed to achieve the most efficient, effective, and safe fire aviation program. The USFS manages flight services procurement of LATs and the DOI manages procurement of the SEATs. Flight services are procured using one of two forms of aircraft contracts; one is an "Exclusive Use" type contract in which the Government contracts for the aircraft, accompanying maintenance, and aircrew for a specified period of time with the exclusive use of the aircraft reserved for the Government. The other form of contract is termed a "Call When Needed" (CWN for the USES) or On-Call for DOI type contract that makes aircraft available to the Government at predetermined rates, if the aircraft is available for service (contingency basis).

Large Type I and Type II fixed wing airtankers have played an increasingly important role in firefighting since the mid-1950s when aircraft were first used to deliver retardant. Today, privately owned airtankers are leased from private operators from February through November and pre-positioned throughout the country based on the fire threat. The number of airtankers currently available to the interagency fire management community is 19.

Type 3 Air Tankers such as CL-215s and Air Tractor 802s will continue to be utilized where available and appropriate. Tactically the mix of CL-215s and the larger SEATs that currently exist are satisfying the requirements of fire operations personnel. Currently, most vendors are moving to larger capacity, turbine driven SEATs, and this is supported by the users in the field. The Type 1 and Type 2 helicopter programs are managed by all federal agencies to varying degrees. Each has the opportunity to contract for these services and does so as needed. The program was first developed to meet the demand for delivery of firefighters, equipment, retardant and suppressants to initial attack and escaped fires. Today, the program is characterized by a high level of competition for the helicopters and an increasing reliance on exclusive use services by some agencies. Many states also have robust helicopter programs supported by the Federal Excess Personal Property (FEPP) program aircraft administered by the U.S. Forest Service.

Question 4d. For example, if a contractor put a bid in to use a Polish PZL-Mielec M-18 Dromader that would meet the contract specifications, would the BLM consider that contractor's bid?

Answer. Any brand type or model of aircraft would be considered if it met the contract specifications for capability, speed, capacity, etc. Contracting of aviation resources from vendors by the USFS and DOT is generally accomplished through Exclusive Use or CWN/OnCall contracts. However, each agency implements its own contracting vehicles that vary in type, language, and format depending upon the type of aviation resource being procured. The diversity of vendors does allow for more flexibility in acquiring aircraft that are a better fit for the geography, fuels, fire behavior, topography and length of season.

The current vendor fleet is provided by a variety of companies, ranging from a vendor with one aircraft to vendors that supply multiple aircraft that are widely distributed across the U.S. This situation makes contract administration, inspections, carding and monitoring of operations more labor and time intensive than contracting with one entity to provide all aircraft, however, when exercised within established doctrine, the use of a variety of aviation resources complements the actions of ground resources, multiplies the effect of those resources on the suppression action, provides a critical margin of safety and lowers total suppression costs.

RESPONSE OF KIM THORSEN TO QUESTION FROM SENATOR BARRASSO

Question 1a. At the public land subcommittee hearing held on May 25111, both Under Secretary Harris Sherman and Deputy Director Marcilynn Burke supported good neighbor authority. In Colorado alone, Mr. Sherman testified the authority has been used successfully on 37 projects covering 3,900 acres. These projects focused on fuel reduction within the wild land-urban interface.

Had my Good Neighbor Forestry Bill been signed into law last year, as it was introduced, would it have aided the forest service in dealing with the terrible forest fuels problems that have been occurring? BLM?

Answer. As noted in our testimony, the Administration supports Good Neighbor Authority, but we believe further study and analysis are needed to better understand the interplay of state and federal contracting and labor law and regulation before expansion of the authority is authorized. We look forward to working with the committee, States, and federal agencies to develop a better understanding of the issues and to improve the bill in a manner that meets the needs of key stakeholders. We welcome opportunities to enhance our capability to manage our natural resources through a landscape-scale approach that crosses a diverse spectrum of land ownerships.

Question 1b. How many more acres might have been treated if Good Neighbor authority was available to the Forest Service? BLM?

Answer. Currently, the BLM has very limited experience with the Good Neighbor authority since the BLM's authority to use it is only in the State of Colorado. BLM Colorado has only completed one project at this time. The number of acres that could have been treated under widespread Good Neighbor authority would depend on the individual state's ability to perform fuels reduction projects and resources available in any given state. Because the BLM only has the authority in Colorado, we have not explored the capacity of other western states to perform fuels reduction treatments and are therefore unable to determine a number of acres that might have been treated.

RESPONSE OF KIM THORSEN TO QUESTION FROM SENATOR HELLER

Question 1. The personal impacts of wildfire are a huge burden to my constituents. I have heard story after story of folks who have watched a fire burn on public lands, been prevented from putting the fire out, only to see it eventually destroy their property.

As you know, if a private party starts a fire that spreads to public lands, they are held accountable. Whereas, if the federal government starts or fails to aggressively suppress a fire that destroys private property—there is vastly less accountability. In light of this, what are the trends in wildland use fires over the last 5 years? And, what percentage of catastrophic wildfires was designated as wildland use fires instead of aggressively suppressed?

Answer. The term "wildland use fires" is no longer used by the federal agencies. With the change in fire policy implementation that occurred in 2009, these fires are now included in the description of fires being managed for "multiple objectives"; which more accurately describes the strategies and tactics of this type of wildfire response.

Wildfires that threaten people, communities or important natural, economic or cultural resources will always be managed for full suppression. The concept of multiple objectives allows fire managers to make decisions based on land and fire management plans. It allows fire to play its natural role where appropriate and focuses suppression efforts in order to protect lives and property. This is in keeping with the principle of having the right response resources at the right place at the right time.

All wildfires receive a response. In appropriate locations that response may be limited to confining a fire within designated boundaries. Where lives and homes are threatened, the response is always full suppression as quickly and efficiently as possible. In some instances, there may be a combination of tactics used on a single fire. Again, this is in line with having the right resources at the right place and right time. It is appropriate to note that when fires are deemed to require aggressive initial attack the overall percentage of success is calculated to be in the positive 95 percentile.

Additionally, there are no criteria for "catastrophic fire," which is a generic description of wildfires that is not used or accepted by the U.S. wildland fire community.

The National Interagency Coordination Center in Boise, Idaho, collects and tracks data from wildfires that are considered "large." By definition, a large fire is one that burns a minimum of 100 acres of primarily forested land or at least 300 acres of rangeland. Given that guideline, in FY 2011, there have been 630 federal large fires, 147 of which have, at one point been managed to achieve multiple objectives.

It is important to note that, in the past, the acreage of multiple objective fires was tracked separately from full-suppression fires. In the last few years, these fire acreages have been lumped into full-suppression fires, as many of them have changed from being managed as full-suppression to multiple objectives and back again. Since management strategies can change, sometimes on a daily basis, it would be ineffective to track these acreages separately.

○

Printed in Great Britain
by Amazon

33080961R00033